EXPLORING CAREERS IN THE NATIONAL PARKS

By
ROBERT GARTNER

The Rosen Publishing Group, Inc.
NEW YORK

Published in 1993, 1997 by The Rosen Publishing Group, Inc.
29 East 21st Street, New York, NY 10010

Copyright 1997 by Robert Gartner

All rights reserved. No part of this book may be reproduced in any form without permission in writing from the publisher, except by a reviewer.

Revised Edition 1997

JOHCA

Library of Congress Cataloging-in-Publication Data

Gartner, Robert.
    Exploring careers in the national parks / by Robert Gartner. — 1st ed.
       p. cm.
    Includes bibliographical references and index.
    Summary: Explores the different careers available within the National Parks Service and offers career tips and information on training.
    ISBN 0-8239-2291-X
    1. National parks and reserves—Vocational guidance—Juvenile literature. 2. National parks and reserves—United States—Vocational guidance—Juvenile literature. 3. United States. National Parks Service—Officials and employees—Juvenile literature. [1. National parks and reserves—Vocational guidance. 2. United States. National Park Service—Vocational guidance. 3. Vocational guidance.] I. Title
SB486.V62G37   1996
363.6'8'02373—dc20   92-39184
                                                                CIP
                                                                 AC

Manufactured in the United States of America

*To Sally and Amy.
Thanks for the constant encouragement and
for making me laugh.*

About the Author

Robert Gartner spent twelve years with the National Park Service in the Washington, D.C., headquarters office, working on planning teams and natural resource programs for wild and scenic rivers, national trails, wilderness, grazing, fisheries, fire, and endangered species. Previously he worked as a park planner for the U.S. Army Corps of Engineers in Fort Worth, Texas, and Savannah, Georgia. He is currently a natural resource specialist for the Bureau of Indian Affairs, and lives in Burke, Virginia.

Gartner has written articles for outdoor publications, technical journals, and newspapers. His book *The National Parks Fishing Guide* was published in 1990.

Acknowledgments

The contributions and dedication of a number of outstanding people have helped turn the idea for this book into a reality. I want to thank the following National Park Service employees for their assistance: Karl Esser, John Townsend, Bill Halainen, Stan Lock, John Reed, Bill Supernaugh, Elmer Hurd, Gary Gregory, Brian Chan, Dave Shea, Sam Swersky, Carol Spears, Jim Lee, Steve Chaney, Ed Bearss, Dan Brown, Ed Trout, Don Pfanz, Terry Winschel, Joan Anzelmo, Cheryl Matthews, Pat Tolle, Larry Belli, Ted Hillmer, Rodney Lowe, Deb Frauson, Lisa Potteboom, Doug Erskine, Butch Farabee, Mary Ingels, John Dill, Walt Dabney, John Coates, Dr. Richard Weisbrod, Brad Traver, Pat Fleming, Anne Frondorf, Ann Hitchcock, Ron Greenburg, Fred Suarez, Bruce Wadlington, Dick Davis, Vergil Noble, Mark Lynott, Dan Lenihan, Dale Ditmanson, Bill Walker, Scott Erickson, Hank Snyder, Tom DuRant, Ric Lewis, Mary Maruca, Barry Mackintosh, Paula Ehrenfeld, Greer Chesher, Bob Schenck, Tom Cherry, Charles Pereira, and Roy Graybill. Thanks also to Wally Elton of the Student Conservation Association, Bob Elmore of the U.S. Forest Service, Joe Helgerson of the Bureau of Indian Affairs, and U.S. Park Police Officers: Deputy Chief Jack Schamp, Major Ed Winkel, Captain Charles Hume, Lt. Ron Schmidt, Lt. Carl Clipper, Captain James McLaughlin, and Sgt. Bernie Stasulli.

Contents

	Introduction	xi
1.	Park Rangers	1
2.	Interpreters	7
3.	Law Enforcement Rangers	19
4.	Superintendent	27
5.	Clerk-Typist: A Stepping-Stone Job	37
6.	United States Park Police	41
7.	Maintenance Workers	55
8.	Backcountry Rangers	65
9.	Park Planners	75
10.	Architects, Engineers, and Landscape Architects	81
11.	Resource Management	87
12.	Scientists	95
13.	Rescue Rangers	101
14.	Historians	109
15.	Archeologists	117
16.	Dispatchers	123
17.	Fire Management	129
18.	Public Affairs Officers	135
19.	Concessions Specialists	145

Contents

20. Training	151
21. Seasonal Employment	157
22. Volunteers in Parks (VIPs)	161
23. Applying for a Federal Government Job	167
24. Career Tips	173

Appendix

1 National Park Service Regional Offices	181
2 Seasonal Law Enforcement Training Program Schools	185
3 Pay Scales	187
For Further Reading	191
Index	193

Introduction

The grizzly roared in pain and outrage as the sharp teeth of the steel trap tore into its leg. The two rangers had finished their patrol and were leading their horses toward camp when they heard the bear's clamor. Forcing their reluctant horses toward the commotion, they reconsidered their careers.

The year was 1916. They had left the U.S. Cavalry to sign on with a new organization, the National Park Service (NPS). The pay was low, the hours were long, and the job was dangerous, but exciting.

Illegal poaching was widespread in the country's few national parks, and rangers constantly patrolled to stop the loss of wildlife caused by hunting and trapping. Arriving at the furious bear they quickly assessed the situation. Should they leave the bear in the trap and hide in an attempt to capture the poacher who had set the trap, or should they do the humane thing and try to free the bear?

Deciding to free the bear, they flipped a coin. The winner had to approach and tease the bear, distracting it while the loser crawled behind the bear and pried open the trap. Once the bear was free, there was a good chance that it would charge its tormentor. Both rangers agreed that it was a no-win situation.

If you decide to become a ranger with the NPS, chances are you will not face such a situation. Ranger jobs and the National Park Service have changed and grown significantly since those early days. This book examines the diverse career opportunities available in some of the most interesting and beautiful sites in the

INTRODUCTION

United States. First, let's consider what the Park Service is all about.

The National Park Service (NPS) is a small but unique agency in the U.S. Department of Interior. The Service has approximately 9,200 permanent employees whose mission is the preservation of irreplaceable resources, including the nation's finest scenery, geologic wonders, and historic treasures. These employees are aided by 11,000 seasonal employees who work during the season when park visitation is heaviest.

The creation of national parks is a distinctly American idea. The world's first national park, Yellowstone, was created in 1872 and marked the beginning of a worldwide movement that has now spread to more than 100 countries.

In 1916, forty-four years after Yellowstone National Park was designated, Congress created the National Park Service. Until 1916, the U.S. Army had been in charge of managing Yellowstone and the handful of other parks established before 1916.

Working for the Park Service is unique because employees regard themselves as "the Service family" and try to promote the family atmosphere. NPS employees are often jokingly referred to as "tree huggers" or "green bloods," but their strong dedication to the parks elevates their work to more than just a job. Some current Park Service employees are descendants of early NPS officials, even extending, in a few cases, to second or third generations.

Ranger Bill Supernaugh grew up in national parks in the West where his father served as a superintendent. One of Bill's career goals is to become superintendent of Joshua Tree National Monument in California, where his father served as superintendent thirty years ago. The Gale family is an example of a third-generation Park Service family. Rick Gale currently

Introduction

works for the Service at the Boise InterAgency Fire Center in Boise, Idaho. His father, Ben Gale, has worked for the Service in a variety of positions and retired as the Deputy Regional Director of the Pacific Northwest Regional Office in Seattle, Washington. Rick's daughter, Beth, is just starting her career as a ranger in Shenandoah National Park in Virginia.

The family concept grows from the fact that many of the parks are in rural or isolated parts of the United States. The families of the Park Service employees depend on each other for many of their social and professional needs. They help each other with the routine facets of everyday life such as child care, shopping, and recreation. Lifelong friendships form among the adults and the children. The common cord binding Park Service employees together in the family feeling is their desire to protect our country's national parks.

Careers with the Park Service are not for clock punchers—those who want to put in their eight hours and go home. During peak seasons, park rangers and staffs work long hours, weekends, and holidays.

The National Park System comprises 361 parks covering 80 million acres in every state except Delaware. Included are parks in the District of Columbia, Guam, Puerto Rico, and the Virgin Islands. Park staffs range in size from seven employees in the smallest area to 630 in Yellowstone at peak season. To support all these parks and provide management guidance, the Park Service maintains a headquarters office in Washington, D.C., and ten regional offices in Boston, Omaha, Anchorage, Philadelphia, Atlanta, Denver, Santa Fe, San Francisco, Seattle, and Washington, D.C.

Many types of areas make up the Park System. Although best known for its great scenic parks, more than half the areas preserve places and commemorate persons, events, and activities important in the nation's

INTRODUCTION

history. Congress has designated a variety of titles to the Park System. In addition to the national parks, the System contains historic sites, battlefields, seashores and lakeshores, national rivers, parkways, and recreation areas, including urban recreation areas.

To give you an idea of the various types of parks in the National Park System, brief definitions and examples follow:

National Park (NP): National parks generally cover a large area containing a variety of resources, and are usually chosen for their natural scenic and scientific values. Yellowstone in Wyoming/Montana/Idaho and Everglades in Florida are prime examples.

National Monument (NM): National monuments generally cover a smaller area than a national park and do not have as great a diversity of attractions. For example, Dinosaur National Monument in Colorado/Utah is an area of archeological significance.

National Seashore (NS)/National Lakeshore (NL): These protect offshore islands and coastal areas and offer water-oriented recreation. National Lakeshores include freshwater areas such as Sleeping Bear Dunes in Michigan; National Seashores include saltwater areas such as Point Reyes in California.

National Historic Park (NHP): A national historic park is an area that preserves the location of an event or activity important to our heritage. The Chesapeake and Ohio Canal (C&O Canal) is an example; it runs through parts of Maryland, West Virginia, and the District of Columbia.

National Historic Site (NHS): A national historic site is similar to a national historic park but is usually smaller, such as the Lyndon B. Johnson Natural Historic Site in Texas, which preserves the former president's birthplace, home, and ranch.

A variety of titles have been used for areas associated

INTRODUCTION

The mission of the National Park Service is to preserve magnificent areas like this, Kings Canyon National Park, for your present and future enjoyment (Richard Frear photo, National Park Service).

with military history: national military park (NMP), national battlefield park (NBP), national battlefield site (NBS), and national battlefield (NB). National monuments and national historical parks may also include features associated with military history.

National Memorial (NMem): These are areas primarily commemorative of a nationally significant individual or event. The Wright Brothers National Memorial in North Carolina and Lincoln Memorial in Washington, D.C., are examples.

National Recreation Area (NRA): This is an area or facility set aside for recreational use. It may include major areas in urban centers. Examples are Lake

INTRODUCTION

Chelan NRA in Washington, a natural area, and Golden Gate NRA in San Francisco, an urban area.

National River (NR) and Wild and Scenic River (WSR): Both of these are free–flowing waterways and include the land along their shores (usually a quarter-mile–wide corridor of land on each side of the river). Buffalo River in Arkansas is a national river and the Obed River in Tennessee is a wild and scenic river.

National Preserve (NPr): A national preserve is an area set aside for the protection of certain natural resources. Big Cypress in Florida and Big Thicket in Texas were the first national preserves.

National Parkway (NPKY): A national parkway is a scenic roadway designed for leisurely driving. The Blue Ridge Parkway in Virginia and North Carolina is representative of the parkways.

The vast size of the System presents diverse job opportunities. This book gives you a sampling of the jobs but couldn't possibly cover all the careers in this eclectic agency. Competition for jobs is keen. The Service employs talented men and women who are comfortable in an urban setting as well as those who prefer the wide open areas. An individual must be well qualified to compete for the permanent full-time positions, because once attained, the Park Service is an agency you can grow with, move within, and stay with for your entire career and always be involved with important and interesting work.

1

Park Rangers

"I love the variety of this job," exclaims John Townsend, former chief ranger at Indiana Dunes National Lakeshore. "Your day is never the same routine. When I was hired, my district ranger told me that each day was a new adventure." Townsend spent one morning overseeing his ranger staff on their park patrols, then four hours in a powerboat on the choppy waters of Lake Michigan rescuing some fishermen whose boat engine had died. Later that night, he fought a fire on park property.

Exciting days that encompass tranquilizing grizzly bears, rescuing stranded climbers, making felony arrests, and firefighting are not unusual to the park ranger. It is just this variety, coupled with the opportunity to help manage 83 million acres of the most magnificent land in the country, that attracts people to ranger careers.

Rangers have always considered themselves a special breed. Comprising 24 percent of the total National Park Service workforce, they are the backbone of the organization. In the formative years of the Service, the first rangers were U.S. Army troopers. Until 1914, the U.S. Cavalry patrolled the Western parks and fought forest fires, built trails, evicted sheepherders, and prevented poachers from killing wildlife. When the National Park Service was created, the Army moved out, but many of the troopers joined the NPS and stayed. These early rangers possessed the discipline and the outdoor skills, resourcefulness, and courage that were essential to the fledgling agency.

Over the years, ranger lineage has striven to maintain the attributes of those original rangers while also adapting to expanded responsibilities as the National Park System grew larger and the Park Service mission continued to evolve. The essence of the ranger was his or her ability to deal with people. As parks became popular vacation spots, the public looked to the ranger to guide and protect them in the wilderness settings. The ranger was expected to tell them all about the wildlife in the park and then protect them from that same wildlife. Soon the ranger was considered one of the natural resources of the parks.

The expansion of the Park System required that ranger skills continue to develop to include "street smarts" for the new urban parks. A ranger in one of the large Western parks can be expected to ride horses, ski, and climb mountains. A ranger in a large urban park such as Gateway National Recreation Area in the New York City area does not need those skills as much as he needs street smarts and crowd control skills. Changing times also require new skills. With today's environmental laws and concerns, all rangers have to deal with ecological issues.

As the ranger's job becomes more complex, the pay scale has not risen to reflect the increased responsibilities. Pay has never been one of the job's attractions. People join the Park Service because they love the parks and working with the public, but overriding that is the belief that they are working to preserve a special national resource.

Butch Farabee, former assistant chief ranger at

The ranger, a symbol of the National Park Service (Bruce Weber photo, National Park Service).

Yosemite National Park in California, recalls, "One year we made almost 600 arrests, and 25 percent were felony arrests. We were facing more danger in a day than FBI agents do in a year, and getting paid half as much." The rangers have a phrase, "surviving on sunsets," to describe their ability to go on without making any financial headway.

A quarter of all rangers are at or below the GS-5 level of the Civil Service pay scale. (See Appendix 3 for an explanation of the pay scale.) The average grade is GS-7.2. To advance beyond the GS-7 level, the ranger usually must become a supervisor, such as a subdistrict ranger. Adding to the frustration is the very low turnover rate above the GS-7 level. Career advancement depends on the number of positions available, and the Park Service has one of the lowest turnover rates in the federal government. The drawback of advancement is that the higher you go, the more time you spend behind a desk and less in actual ranger duties.

Typical advancement for a ranger is to become a subdistrict ranger, then a district ranger. The next move might be a division chief position in a park, such as chief of interpretation, chief of visitor protection, or chief ranger, and from there to park superintendent. In between some of these steps time may be spent in the regional offices or Washington D.C., headquarters. From superintendent, rangers may move to top management positions, such as associate regional director for operations, or associate director of headquarters.

Most rangers emphasize the positive aspects of their job and hope the negative aspects improve. Many rangers are not concerned with advancement and its attendant administrative duties, but are happy to continue in a job and place that they love. Some rangers with a historical bent only seek jobs in other historical parks; others try to move every few years from one scenic park to another, getting to know our country's great scenic attractions.

In 1977 the rangers formed the Association of National Park Rangers (ANPR) to promote and enhance the profession and its spirit. Each year in the fall, ANPR gathers for a Ranger Rendezvous, bringing together 500 to 600 rangers to renew old friendships, make new friends, and discuss mutual job concerns. The meeting is philosophically linked to the annual rendezvous of the trappers and mountain men in the West in the 1800s. The rangers travel on their own time and pay expenses for themselves and their families. The rendezvous is held at resort areas throughout the country.

There will never be a shortage of rangers. Despite the generally low pay and often risky and adverse working conditions, former Park Service Director William Penn Mott once observed, "There are people waiting in the wings for every job."

2

Interpreters

Interpretive rangers deserve considerable credit for shaping the public's favorable image of the National Park Service. The rangers giving the campfire talk, leading the nature walk, or explaining the battle's turning point are part of each park's interpretation staff. They meet the public every day, taking the essence of the park's resources and unveiling it to the public. The visitor leaves the park happy, having learned something new and experienced something meaningful.

Interpretation in the national parks does not mean translating information from one language to another. The definition of the term was formulated by the late Freeman Tilden, known as the Father of Interpretation. Tilden defined interpretation as an educational activity that aims to reveal meanings and relationships through the use of original objects by firsthand experience and illustrative media, rather than simply to communicate factual information.

What interpretation boils down to is telling the story of each park and the National Park Service. Through park brochures, videos, slide presentations, printed information, and personal, well-polished presentations, visitors learn about the national parks.

Interpretive rangers do not have a standard presentation that they give in every park. Each park has dozens of programs, and new ones are always being developed.

The national parks offer a vast array of subjects to interpret, from Civil War battlefields at Gettysburg (Pennyslvania) and Shiloh (Tennessee), ancient Indian cultures at Chaco Culture National Historic Park (New Mexico), magnificent scenic vistas at Yosemite (California) and Rocky Mountain (Colorado), to barrier island formation at Cape Hatteras National Seashore (North Carolina).

Each park has a distinct reason for existence, and guiding rangers is the Statement for Interpretation. The statement describes the resources or events for which the park was established and directs the development of all interpretive programs in that park. Each program must relate to the Statement for Interpretation and develop the specific resources or historical events in that park.

Interpretive rangers must possess a basic ability to communicate with people of all backgrounds and ages. Interpreters speak daily in front of large groups of people, which is not always easy. Many people dislike public speaking. Organizations such as Toastmasters International can help a person become more comfortable with it, and usually speakers improve with experience. But if you do not like to speak before crowds, interpretation is not for you.

Assume you are a new interpreter at a park. Where do you start? The first thing to do at any park is to immerse yourself in its resources and learn as much as possible. Carol Spears is chief of interpretation at Channel Islands National Park in California. She is also a former recipient of the annual Freeman Tilden Award for interpretive innovation and excellence. According to Carol, "Learning about the resources is not enough. Good interpreters must understand and love the resources in their own way and share that love and understanding with the visitors. You are sharing yourself, but the primary focus must remain on the resource."

Sam Swersky is an interpreter at Glen Echo Park in Washington, D.C. He formerly worked at the Custis-Lee Mansion in Arlington National Cemetery and at the White House. Sam repeats Carol's convictions. "You really have to have a love for the park," he says. "From that love comes a fervor for preserving your park and conveying that message to your audience."

Part of Sam's immersion in the resource at the Custis-Lee Mansion was a ten-day tour of the house and grounds with the house curator. "For ten days I basically lived in the house, learning the historic events that happened there," Sam explained. "Each historic park has a way of bringing history to life. No matter where you are standing, you can recount what happened at that spot." During his tour of the Mansion, Sam learned about the events in every room, including the room where General Lee agonized over his decision to turn down a commission with the Union Army and join the Confederate forces. "These bits of historic drama humanize a house," said Sam. "Otherwise you are just displaying a house with rooms full of old furniture."

Besides doing extensive research on the park and the surrounding area, interpreters need to understand the National Park Service role in preserving that park. What would the area look like now if not for the Park Service? One need only look at the shopping malls and housing developments encroaching on existing national parks. Part of the interpreters' message is the pivotal role played by the Park Service in preserving the area.

After a short immersion in the park's history and resources, the new interpreter starts developing programs in concert with the Statement for Interpretation.

In developing programs, interpreters follow Freeman Tilden's six principles of interpretation:

1. Any interpretation that does not somehow relate what is being displayed or described to something within the personality or experience of the visitor will be sterile.
2. Information as such is not interpretation. Interpretation is revelation based upon information. However, all interpretation includes information.
3. Interpretation is an art that combines many arts, whether the materials presented are scientific, historical, or architectural. Any art is in some degree teachable.
4. The chief aim of interpretation is not instruction but provocation.
5. Interpretation should aim to present a whole rather than a part and must address itself to the whole man rather than any phase.
6. Interpretation addressed to children (up to twelve years old) should not be a dilution of the presentation to adults, but should follow a fundamentally different approach. To be at its best, it requires a separate program.

These principles are taken from Tilden's book *Interpreting Our Heritage*, which Carol describes as "the Bible of interpretation."

In creating a program, the interpreter develops an outline defining the theme, the goals, and the audience. Determining the best method of presentation is the next step. Should the program include a hike, demonstrations, hands-on displays, or a game? There are numerous ways to get the point across, and with experience you learn to match the message with the best presentation method. The interpreter first works out these details with the supervisor. When the program is ready, the supervisor audits it, providing feedback and making suggestions for improvement.

The famous campfire talks, the nature hikes, the battlefield walks, and other presentations are not random events. Each program is well prepared.

The campfire talks are always popular, coming after dark when visitor activities are limited. Tonight's program is about wildlife. The interpretive ranger introduces a few typical animals and gives some basic information about them. The talk then relates the animals to their environment and to each other so that interrelationships are evident.

The audience's interest is piqued. They had expected an entertaining talk on wildlife, and they're getting much more. The ranger has them thinking how individual animals affect or are affected by each other, by the soils and plants growing about them, and by the climate and the seasons.

The talk includes pointers on how and where to observe wildlife and some of the wildlife problems occurring in the park. The ranger discusses the complexities of wildlife management and explains the park's wildlife policy, concluding with the philosophy of national parks and their intangible values.

At program's end, the ranger has led the audience through a realm of thought far beyond routine information about park animals. The ecological approach has informed and entertained them, and they leave having learned a lot about wildlife and about the Park Service and its policies.

The campfire talk is typical of a Park Service interpretive program. You always get more than you expected, and the program is not presented as a grimly purposeful educational lecture. Most park visitors are on vacation

EXPLORING CAREERS IN THE NATIONAL PARKS

An interpretive talk at Sequoia/Kings Canyon National Parks (Richard Frear photo, National Park Service).

and not inclined to sit through such a lecture. In reality, they are being educated along the way, often without knowing it.

There is a vast amount of information to convey at each park, and interpreters are aware that the visitors' enjoyment of a presentation can suffer from information overload. "We know we can't tell the entire story, so we try to whet their appetite for more information," explains Sam.

Interpretation includes the use of publications and exhibits to complement face-to-face programs. Movies, slide shows, videotapes, brochures, handbooks, trail guides, and wayside exhibits are all valuable tools.

Each park has a visitor center, which features interpretive exhibits and programs and a selection of books, videos, and slides about the park specifically and the Park Service in general. Through the interpretive programs and displays, you can get a feeling for the park resources and focus your visit on areas of interest to you. The visitor centers are great resources for learning more about the park.

Another reason for stopping at a visitor center is to obtain a schedule of the interpretive programs. Rangers at historic parks often steer visitors to the living history demonstrations, which are popular during the summer and on weekends during the rest of the year. A living history program features interpreters dressed in period clothing, demonstrating daily life or crafts at that time in history. Civil War battlefields may have interpreters clad in Confederate uniforms demonstrating camp life and cooking a typical camp meal. George Washington's Birthplace National Monument in Virginia has men and women dressed in Colonial clothing making candles or dyeing wool. Visitors often participate in these hands-on demonstrations and leave the park with an appreciation for the difficulties of living without our modern conveniences. These programs often depend on seasonal employees and Volunteers in Parks (VIPS).

As in other disciplines, interpreters receive special training. The Park Service offers four core courses totaling 200 training hours on basic interpretive skills. The courses cover the entire gamut of an interpreter's work, from serving the public at the visitor center desk to writing for exhibits and publications, to special programs and audiences.

In addition, specialized courses are given on interpreting military resources and Native American cultures, and on planning an interpretive program.

I have participated in some interpretive training courses by presenting a natural resource problem to the class and asking them to develop a program to educate the public on the problem. The class would divide into teams of six, each addressing a different problem. Each team would research the problem and develop an interpretive program to present to the class at the end of the five-day course.

One year I presented the problem of the declining wild steelhead trout populations in Olympic National Park. We discussed the reasons for the decline, such as increased commercial harvesting in the ocean. We also examined the problems of habitat degradation from extensive logging, which contributes to erosion, causing silt to cover the spawning beds and smother the eggs. The team did additional research and talked to park biologists and Washington State fisheries biologists. They developed a program that explained the steelhead's importance to the region and the ecology of the park; the reasons for its decline and the steps needed to reverse the trend; a campaign aimed at fishermen, promoting catch and release of wild steelhead, including a small illustrated card showing the differences between a wild steelhead and one raised in a hatchery; and

INTERPRETERS

An interpretive hike at Yellowstone National Park (T & N Ramhorse photo, National Park Service).

the Park Service policy on fishing and preserving native populations. It was an impressive and effective program. The class learned the process of identifying and researching a problem and developing an interpretive response, just as it is done in the parks.

No matter how many training classes you take, the best trainer of all is the public. Formal training is only for a week or two at a time, but the interpreter is with the public every day and through experience finds the subject or type of presentation that holds people's attention. Every interpreter has a failure sometime. People leave during the presentation or are glassy-eyed when it's over. Their body language screams: BORING! The key is to learn from failures and constantly improve.

"Knowing that you got your point across and the audience loved the program is what an interpreter lives for," says Carol. "My biggest thrill is seeing the gleam in someone's eyes when they understand the importance of the park." Sam echoes her feelings. "I want the visitor to leave as enthused about the park as I am," he says. "The biggest compliment I receive is to have someone come back and bring a friend to one of my programs."

When former President George Bush visited Grand Canyon National Park in 1991, interpreter Greer Chesher led him and some Cabinet members on a hike. "Actually the President led us," Greer explains. "He was far ahead of everybody, and we had to hustle to keep up." She was with the President for an hour, answering his questions and telling him about the history of the canyon. "Most of his questions were about me, my family, and my parents," she says. "Where was I from? Did I have children? Where did my parents live? It was fun and intimidating, but I was honored to be asked to guide him."

Former President Jimmy Carter had a favorite interpreter at Gettysburg Battlefield. The Presidential retreat at Camp David, Maryland, is only thirty minutes away. On his first trip to Gettysburg, the President was accompanied by the noted Civil War historian Shelby Foote, and his press secretary, Jody Powell. Interpreter Robert Prosperi was assigned to lead them on a battlefield tour. On his next trip, President Carter brought Egyptian President Anwar Sadat with him and requested that Bob Prosperi be their guide.

Spending time with presidents is not part of an interpreter's normal day. About half the day is spent with the public; program preparation and ancillary duties take up the rest. Many interpreters are also Volunteers in Parks (VIP) coordinators. Administrative duties such as maintaining slide files and audiovisual programs eat into the day. "My biggest frustration is not having enough time to do more research," says Sam. Carol voices a similar complaint. "I would like more time to prepare because I want to give the best presentation possible."

Depending on the park, the interpreter may not have enough time to spend with the public. Heavy visitation results in too many people and too little time to enjoy the post-presentation mingling and discussions. Interpreters at popular parks often give many presentations throughout the day and when finishing one program quickly start another.

The positive aspects of hosting so many visitors is the opportunity to create new advocates for the national parks. Interpreters annually educate millions of people about our nation's scenic, natural, and cultural treasures. "Our goal in creating interpretive programs is to educate the public," says Carol. "We want them to take away at least one nugget of information every time they visit a park." Besides the nugget of information carried away, visitors leave with a good feeling for the National Park Service.

3

Law Enforcement Rangers

A law enforcement ranger is a policeman whose beat is the scenic and historic landscapes of the United States rather than a city's streets. The primary goal of the law enforcement ranger is to protect the park visitors, park resources, and park property. In many instances, the rangers protect the visitor from the resource and the resource from the visitor. Law enforcement rangers, like those in natural resources and interpretation, have a number of responsibilities. They may also be responsible for emergency medical services, environmental compliance, wildland and structural fire suppression, and criminal investigations.

To perform law-enforcement duties, a ranger needs a law-enforcement commission. To receive a commission, the ranger must complete a training program at the Federal Law Enforcement Training Center (FLETC) in Glynco, Georgia.

Bill Supernaugh is the former superintendent of the Park Service's training program at FLETC. Earlier in his career, Bill was a law enforcement ranger on the Natchez Trace Parkway and the Blue Ridge Parkway. He took a break from his new position as assistant superintendent at Indiana Dunes National Lakeshore to explain the commissioning process to me.

There are two types of NPS law-enforcement commissions, Level I and Level II. The Level I Commission, held by most permanently employed rangers, grants the greater authority. Rangers are eligible for it upon graduating from a ten-week training course entitled, "Basic Law Enforcement for Land Management Agencies." About 130 to 150 rangers graduate from this course every year. Candidates must pass a background investigation and must be recommended by their superintendent. "You're looking for a person who can handle stress and be even-handed in encounters with the public," Supernaugh emphasizes.

During the FLETC course, the rangers receive training in criminal and civil law; human relations skills; enforcement techniques such as surveillance, execution of search warrants, and violent-death investigations; scientific and technological skills such as fingerprinting, crime scene photography, and the collection and preservation of evidence; officer safety and survival; motor vehicle driving skills, including courses in skid control and pursuit driving; firearms training; and physical training including arrest and control techniques and defensive skills against armed and unarmed persons.

Within these general categories is intensive specialized training. Realism is important in teaching, and the course employs professional role players and carefully designed scenarios to teach the class by practical examples.

Following graduation, a ranger is eligible to be issued a Level I law-enforcement commission from the regional office. In 1990 a total of 1,523 rangers in the Park Service held Level I commissions.

Level II commissions are generally held by seasonal rangers who have taken basic training on their own in an effort to land a job with the Park Service. Level II commissions are earned by taking a minimum of 280 hours of law-enforcement training from one of the twenty-two universities throughout the country that provide it. (See Appendix 2 for a list of these schools.) Bill says, "Nearly every job applicant holding a Level II commission gets a seasonal job with the Park Service, usually as a GS-4 ranger." Some 900 rangers hold Level II commissions.

Rangers with Level II commissions can carry firearms, make arrests, investigate motor vehicle accidents (except fatalities), investigate violations of the Code of Federal Regulations, and take initial reports on felonies or fatalities.

The Level II commission differs from Level I in the degree of investigative responsibility. Level II rangers may not serve warrants or investigate felonies, death, or serious injuries. They may help with these activities but may not take a leading role. According to Supernaugh, "Seasonal rangers are here today and gone tomorrow, and many of these investigations take a year or more to bring to trial. For the sake of continuity, the Service requires a Level I commissioned ranger to take the lead."

If a seasonal ranger with a Level II commission lands a permanent position with the Park Service, his limited commission can be used for up to two years while awaiting the FLETC training program.

The training does not end when a ranger gains a law-enforcement commission. All rangers at both levels must receive forty hours of refresher training each year and must qualify with their firearms twice a year. The regional offices generally sponsor the refresher courses for their parks. The refresher course covers any new legal decisions that affect the Park Service; any changes in Park Service policy or new guidelines affecting law enforcement, and an introduction to pertinent new techniques or skills.

Serious felonies are uncommon in the parks, but they do occur. Rangers have been assaulted and injured, and the risks have increased with the growth of the drug culture. Drug dealers grow marijuana on public lands because of what they stand to lose if they grow it on their own land: Federal agents can confiscate the land and house of anyone caught growing marijuana at home. So the dealers seek out secluded areas of national parks and forests to raise their illegal crop. They usually booby-trap the area around their plot, posing a risk to both rangers and visitors who inadvertently stumble onto it.

Traffic control and crimes involving cars are a constant problem. Directing traffic, arresting drunk drivers, and dealing with vehicle accidents occupies a good part of the ranger's day. Drunk drivers are especially lethal on the twisting, narrow roads typical of most parks. In Yosemite National Park, bumper-to-bumper traffic is a way of life. Accompanying the gridlock are innumerable fender benders and overheated tempers. The ranger must sort all this out and keep cool in the face of testy tourists.

Thieves strike quickly as they cruise the park looking for cars parked in remote areas or at a trailhead. They break in and steal cameras, cash, and credit cards. Vandalism of parked cars, known as "car clouting," continues to be a problem.

Like other police officers, law enforcement rangers develop a sixth sense about situations and people. Cops call it "street smarts." In Texas, Big Bend National Park ranger Kathy Hambly helped some visitors whose motor home was stuck. The vehicle was soon freed, and the visitors gratefully continued on their way. Something struck Kathy as "not quite right" about the incident, however, and she took down identifying information about the motor home and its occupants.

LAW ENFORCEMENT RANGERS

Ranger checking fish on Yellowstone Lake (National Park Service).

After passing that information on to the Border Patrol, she went back to the scene and traced the vehicle's tracks back to the Mexican border, where it intersected with three sets of horse tracks. Knowing that this kind of rendezvous is a common practice of drug dealers, she notified the Border Patrol again, giving them enough information to stop the motor home about 50 miles north of the park. The Patrol searched the vehicle and found 663 pounds of cocaine, with an estimated street value of $148 million.

Most law-enforcement incidents in parks involve resource violations. Organized poaching operations illegally kill big-game animals such as bear, elk, moose, deer, and bighorn sheep. There is a strong underground market for the meat and body parts of these animals, especially in the Orient, where deer and elk antlers are used as aphrodisiacs. Bear gallbladders are in demand for their supposed healing powers. Poachers kill the bear, rip out the gallbladder, maybe cut off the paws for a Chinese food delicacy, and leave the rest for vultures.

Park vegetation is stolen for landscaping uses. Rhododendrons are especially popular. Bark is stripped from yew trees in the Pacific Northwest and used for herbal potions and a new experimental cancer treatment. Mushrooms, both rare and common, are collected and sold for huge profits.

The bane of historic parks is the relic hunter. Armed with metal detectors, scavengers hit a battlefield park at night digging for guns, eating utensils, bullets, whatever treasures they can unearth and sell. Last year more than a million tourists visited the four battlefields that make up the Fredericksburg and Spotsylvania County National Military Park. Rangers cited forty-three violations of laws protecting the park resources. Thirteen people were prosecuted and convicted. Many relic hunters do

Law Enforcement Rangers

not realize they are breaking the law by prospecting on national park property. Conversely, the relic hounds plot their forays into the park, and if caught and sentenced are often back in action after serving the typical ten to twenty days in jail.

Fighting back, the rangers increase their patrols, identify frequent incident areas, and mount sting operations. Wildlife poaching is a constant problem in parks like Shenandoah and Great Smoky Mountains, where the rings prey on deer and black bear. Park rangers work closely with the U.S. Fish and Wildlife Service (FWS) and state game wardens to break these rings.

In Shenandoah National Park, the rangers launched an operation known as "Little Debbie Raisin Cakes." Several groups of poachers were placing dozens of Little Debbie raisin cakes in the woods to attract deer. A ranger apprehended a poacher, who cooperated with the Park Service and the FWS to place an undercover agent in the poaching ring. Forty-five people were arrested when the ring was smashed. Rangers estimated that 400 deer per year were being killed.

Rangers also have to protect the resources from well-meaning visitors. Camera-laden tourists abandon good sense and try to get closer to wild animals than the law allows. It seems that every year a visitor at Yellowstone walks up to a grazing buffalo and puts an arm across the animal's shoulders while someone snaps a photo or films the action with a video camera. Often the pictures and film are developed to reveal the visitor being stomped or gored by an enraged buffalo.

In the campgrounds, campers store their food carelessly, inviting the bears to pay nocturnal scavenging visits and leading to potentially dangerous encounters. In cases where a visitor is killed or injured, the bear may have to be destroyed.

Every day the law enforcement rangers cope with this

juggling act of protecting visitors, resources, and property. When you have locked your keys in your car, misplaced a child, twisted an ankle, dented a bumper, broken a bone, or lost your wallet, nothing is more reassuring than a ranger's presence.

4

Superintendent

Without a doubt, the most coveted title in the Park Service is "park superintendent." Park superintendents are an elite group of more than 300 men and women who are in charge of our national parks.

The majority of superintendents come from the ranks of rangers, usually law enforcement, interpretation, or resource management. The system has opened, however, to snare qualified candidates from other park backgrounds such as maintenance and administration.

Superintendents attain the position after long years of working their way up through the ranks, taking on more responsibility, and demonstrating their management ability. The rangers call the process "paying your dues." Dues-paying often involves less-than-desirable assignments in isolated parks or at regional or headquarters offices. Assignment to a regional office can be pure misery to rangers accustomed to the uncrowded rural lifestyle where you know your neighbors and can leave your car unlocked. In these positions, however, they learn the overall picture of managing parks and how policies affect the entire National Park System. Whatever form it takes, most superintendents pay dues sometime during their career.

Depending on the size of the park, superintendents function a bit differently. Superintendents of large parks such as Great Smoky Mountains, Everglades,

Yellowstone, Yosemite, and Grand Canyon have an assistant superintendent (AS). In small to medium parks, the superintendent goes it alone.

In a large park, the superintendent usually spends the most time working on issues or threats from outside the park that could harm its resources or impair visitors' enjoyment. In these parks, the assistant superintendent often runs the day-to-day operations. Each situation is different, and the real effectiveness of an AS is often determined by how well he or she gets along with the boss, the superintendent. The superintendent is like the chairman of the board, operating outside park boundaries to secure a stable future for the park, whereas the assistant superintendent acts as the chief executive officer, the person making the daily management decisions.

Superintendent Dale Enquist of Indiana Dunes National Lakeshore put it well when he greeted his new assistant superintendent, Bill Supernaugh: "Think of the two of us standing at the park boundary. I'll look outside the park and take care of everything happening out there. You look inside the park and take care of everything happening in here."

Although the superintendent is kept busy dealing with national and local issues, he may have a special interest in certain programs, such as concessions or resource management, and may keep them under his direct supervision. The superintendent usually handles land acquisition matters, working with local people or government agencies to swap or acquire land parcels that will benefit the overall management of the park. He may work with park planners to direct development through the General Management Plan (GMP). He may deal with zoning boards to protect the park boundaries from commercial or residential development. Shopping centers, gas stations, or manufacturing plants are often proposed for construction adjacent to park lands. These forms of progress would totally alter the historic scene or damage the natural habitat of the park's wildlife.

Shenandoah National Park superintendent Bill Wade is upset by the haze of pollution, much of it carried by wind from smokestacks in West Virginia and the Ohio Valley. Shenandoah's scenic vistas, one of its main attractions, are obscured by the increased air pollution. Wade has thrust himself into the controversies over real estate development and air pollution outside the park because these issues have an effect on what happens inside the park.

In the days before air pollution became noticeable, before acid rain and development along park boundaries, superintendents could concentrate on what was happening inside the park. Today they often don't have that luxury. National parks are being threatened on all sides, forcing superintendents to think about the park's relationship with surrounding localities and the state.

Geothermal mining interests want to drill outside the boundary of Yellowstone National Park. What effect will this have on the boiling mudpots and the geysers, especially Old Faithful, the most famous geyser of all? Will the drilling vent the underground pressure and ruin the geysers? No one knows. The superintendent is fighting the drilling interests until studies are completed showing how drilling would affect the park's geothermal resources.

The great sport fishing grounds of Florida Bay in Everglades National Park were being depleted by commercial fishermen. Redfish, snook, and sea trout populations dropped to dangerously low levels. Ton after ton of these fish ended their lives in a trawl net. Superintendent Jack Morehead used his authority to protect the park resources and phased out commercial fishing in 1985. Since then, the fishery has rebounded.

Besides fighting the threats to the parks, superintendents often deal with various political entities. Some parks have twenty or more—they include local officials, county commissioners, mayors, state representatives, and national congresspeople. It is vital to have good rapport with the national delegation, the U.S. Senators, and members of the House of Representatives; they are the ones who steer funding to the park for increased programs and special projects.

When congresspeople visit a park, the superintendent is their personal tour guide and insures that they leave with a good impression of the park and its staff. Presidents, accompanied by Cabinet members or visiting heads of state, also come to the parks. Before such a visit, the superintendent and the ranger staff work closely with the Secret Service to guarantee the President's safety. Much time and effort is expended preparing for a Presidential visit. Superintendents can spend months working with the Secret Service, preparing for a visit that may last an hour or half a day.

A necessary part of occupying the top job is making the tough, controversial decisions. Many decisions are not always popular, and the superintendent may be pressured by political interests. Concessioners have used political connections to try to influence decisions. Mining companies want to explore inside park boundaries. Those are some of the problems touched on earlier as threats to the parks, but the superintendent is the one who must defend the park's integrity and make the often unpopular decisions.

Two controversial decisions that come to mind are the reintroduction of wolves into Yellowstone National Park and the removal of burros from Death Valley and Grand Canyon National Parks.

The reintroduction of the gray wolf to Yellowstone is part of a recovery plan to help this endangered species.

SUPERINTENDENT

It is hoped that the wolves will establish themselves in the park and increase their populations. Gray wolves were routinely killed in Yellowstone during the 1930s, a period when wolves and other predators were eliminated as a national policy. Wolves were released into the park in 1995, but the Park Service still faces opposition from ranchers near the park who fear that the wolves will prey upon their livestock.

The burro issue was controversial because animal rights groups protested the killing of burros in the parks. The burros are exotic animals in the parks, meaning that they are not native, and they caused considerable damage to park resources. Animal rights groups protested the Park Service's plan to kill the burros and were offered the opportunity to remove the animals at their own expense. The parks even sponsored an "Adopt a Burro" program to encourage the public to remove them. Congressmen were bombarded with letters that disapproved of the killing of these "gentle creatures." Despite the uproar, the superintendents of both parks stuck to their decision.

Burros are among nature's vandals, creating serious erosion problems. The trails made by their wanderings through both parks will be evident for at least twenty years. They also displace native animals, particularly bighorn sheep. Burros may look lovable and cuddly, but their presence creates a management problem.

When Gil Lusk was superintendent of Glacier National Park in Montana, he made a decision that was not especially controversial but was surprising because it was not traditional. A wildlife photographer was mauled to death by a grizzly bear sow in the park. Gil decided that the bear should not be killed. Generally, when a bear kills a human, it is tracked down and killed, especially if the animal has a history of aggressive behavior toward humans. Once a bear kills a human and realizes how easy it is, the chances are good that it will kill again.

In this case, however, the situation was different. Photographs developed from the dead man's film showed that he was the aggressor, not the bear. The photographer had pursued the bear and her cubs, causing her to react instinctively to protect her young. After killing the photographer in defense, the bear showed no interest in the body of the victim. Lusk evaluated the evidence and decided that no action should be taken against the bear.

While the superintendents at the large parks are wrestling with threats to the park and doing their political groundwork, what is the assistant superintendent doing? The AS is the director behind the scenes, and is managing daily operations. The various park divisions—maintenance, resource management, law enforcement, interpretation—receive their marching orders from the AS. He also handles the budget, as well as hiring and administrative duties, such as correspondence and employee performance evaluations. Internal problems are resolved in his office. When the superintendent is out of the park, the AS is the acting superintendent.

It seems like an enviable position, and it can be a good career move if the superintendent is a good trainer, a mentor who will share his or her years of experience and help the AS toward a superintendency. The position is also an opportunity to find out if the AS is suited for management.

One assistant superintendent recommends caution before accepting an AS position. "If you think the AS post is a door to a superintendency, go for it, but be aware that you could get trapped in the position." Some rangers have spent ten years in the AS post and failed to be tapped for superintendent vacancies in other parks. The

Park Service seems to have an unwritten rule that the AS is never appointed to the superintendent position in the same park. Supposedly it is not good for the park. I fail to see the logic behind this philosophy, but the Park Service nearly always holds to it. The best analogy I've heard is that the AS is like a midwife who delivers the babies and lances the boils but someone else has the title "Doctor."

How about a small park that doesn't have the benefit of an assistant superintendent? What does the superintendent do? "Everything," answers Larry Belli. "You're involved in every aspect of park management." Larry is superintendent of Chaco Culture National Historic Park in New Mexico. He supervises a staff of forty. Chaco is his first superintendency. He worked as a law enforcement ranger, then as a resource management specialist at Glen Canyon National Recreation Area in Arizona and Utah, and then worked in the Ranger Activities Division in Washington, D.C.

A superintendency at a small park is an important stepping-stone to the better-paid and more visible superintendencies at larger parks. The superintendent has the same responsibilities as the head of a large park, and he also runs the day-to-day operations.

In his role as head man, Larry sees three primary functions for himself. The first is gaining new funding for park projects. Be it funds for road construction, additional interpretive staff, or office computers, each superintendent has to compete against others for the limited funds available for park projects and programs. The trick, once you get additional funds, is keeping them year after year.

The second main function is setting priorities for the park staff and communicating goals to them. "It is essential for the staff to have priorities, direction, and goals so that everyone knows their role in the successful management of the park," Larry says. "To be successful, you have to know your staff and their individual capabilities. Putting the right people in the right jobs is the key to success."

Larry's third function is to monitor the priorities and direction to see that the goals are accomplished. "If priorities get off track, fix the situation immediately," he emphasizes.

A superintendent at a small park has to understand how a park functions and how each division complements the others and contributes to a smoothly running park. Larry cautions against micromanagement. "Let your division chiefs run their programs. If I've set priorities, they know what I want. A superintendent doesn't have time to get involved in every decision; besides, you have to let your division chiefs develop their own management skills."

In small parks, the superintendent develops the budget and is more involved in personnel matters. Is the park operating efficiently on the current budget? What would happen if the budget were increased by a certain percentage? Conversely, what would happen if the budget were cut by the same percentage? The superintendent has to have a thorough understanding of the budget and what can be accomplished with the allocated funds. Superintendents at the large parks usually have the AS or a budget specialist on staff to handle the budget. Larry doesn't have that luxury, nor does he want it. "If you are going to be successful, you have to understand the budget process," he states. "Once you learn the process, it remains the same, no matter the size of the park."

Larry also recommends learning about personnel issues such as hiring, position descriptions, and annual evaluations. Personnel work is not popular with the majority of superintendents because it takes a lot of time and paperwork. Spending a day rewriting a position description or completing written performance evaluations is not fun, but it is necessary.

In small parks, the division chiefs make the hiring selections for vacancies, but the superintendent reserves the right to approve them. In contrast, the superintendent at a large park like Yellowstone selects people for vacancies on his management staff but is less inclined to get involved with other positions, instead leaving the decisions to the division chiefs.

Small parks are good training grounds for first-time superintendents. They can further develop their skills and thoroughly learn how a park operates. As a superintendent's career advances from small to large park, the arena changes but the job remains the same: protect the parks for the present and future enjoyment of the public.

5

Clerk-Typist: A Stepping-Stone Job

Clerk-typist? Isn't that a fancy name for a secretary? Isn't the secretary the lowest person on the totem pole? What chance do I have to advance in my career if I take a job as a secretary?

You may ask yourself these questions before you apply for a job as a clerk-typist. Yes, "clerk-typist" is a government term for "secretary." I shall refer to clerk-typists as secretaries throughout this description.

There is also a common perception that secretarial positions are held only by women. Twenty years ago that may have been the case, but today a number of men hold secretary positions in the Park Service.

Secretarial jobs are no longer considered "dead end" positions. Many people use the job as an entrance into the National Park Service to gain experience and then advance. Lorraine Mintzmeyer started as a secretary and, over the years, advanced to become superintendent at two parks and finally a Regional Director. In the fall of 1995, Karen Brown became superintendent at Abraham Lincoln Birthplace National Historic Site in Hodgenville, Kentucky. Karen began her career in 1979 at Cuyahoga Valley National Recreation Area in Ohio as a clerk-typist. By moving and advancing in other positions, Karen was ready for her first superintendency.

Any supervisor will tell you that a good secretary is worth his or her weight in gold. A secretary may be the lowest-paid person in an office but he or she is indispensable. In Washington, D.C., a good secretary can always find a job; in fact, the government has a hard time retaining secretaries. Private businesses and law firms frequently raid the government for the best secretaries by offering better salaries and benefits than the government can provide.

What do secretaries do and what skills do they need? Obviously, one's typing ability is the most important skill. The basic job of a secretary is to produce clean, error-free letters and reports. In today's office, paperwork and correspondence are done on computers using word processing programs such as WordPerfect, Microsoft Word, or Word Star. The federal government uses WordPerfect.

Upwardly mobile secretaries use every opportunity to learn other computer software such as database, spreadsheet, and graphics programs. The more computer application skills one acquires, the more job opportunities will be available.

People skills are as important as typing skills. People skills for secretaries include the ability to deal with a variety of personalities, maintain your cool, and make the person feel better for having worked with you. Good people skills will help you advance in any job. These skills are often put to the test in taking phone calls and messages for your coworkers. Answering phones is a thankless but essential duty. Your ability to talk intelligently to people and accurately record and relay their messages relieves a lot of the caller's frustration when the person wanted isn't available.

My office lost a great secretary to a lobbying firm because the firm was impressed by the way she an-

Clerk-Typist: A Stepping-Stone Job

swered the phone. Each time the lobbyists called our office, the call went through the secretary, who would either connect the caller or take a message if the party was out. When a vacancy arose at the lobbying firm, they called our secretary to ask her to apply for the vacancy. She was offered the job at her first interview.

As you advance as a secretary, you take on more responsibilities. Usually you advance in salary (grade) by moving up to the secretarial position at the next management level. As an example, a secretary in a ranger district office becomes a secretary for the Branch of Law Enforcement and then moves up to Division Secretary for Ranger Activities, and finally to secretary for the superintendent.

Some of these new responsibilities include setting up meetings. The meetings may be with just park staff or they may be with staff and some of the townspeople. The secretary may be expected to take notes, or minutes, of the meeting and write a meeting summary. In a regional or headquarters office, the secretary may arrange statewide or national meetings. The logistics of national meetings include selecting the meeting site, reserving blocks of hotel rooms, arranging catering, scheduling the program, contacting speakers, and providing audiovisual equipment.

The "clerk" part of clerk-typist usually refers to sorting and delivering the mail and maintaining the files. The secretary also determines which staffperson should receive or respond to incoming letters and information.

Every piece of government correspondence has a file code on it pertaining to the subject. Secretaries also file each piece of correspondence in its specific file folder. That doesn't sound too exciting, but the secretary is knowledgeable about every piece of correspondence entering or leaving an office and thus learns about the park's business, issues, or controversies. This knowledge is always useful and may open new career paths. As one superintendent said, "If you call me and I'm not in, ask my secretary any questions you may have. She knows more about how this park runs than I do."

Secretaries also make travel arrangements, including flight, rental car, and hotel reservations. When the travelers return, they usually give their rental car, hotel, and parking receipts to the secretary; travel vouchers are completed and sent to the financial office, which will then reimburse the traveler for certain expenses incurred while on government travel.

Secretaries are often considered the office manager, as well. They administer the day-to-day activities necessary to keep an office operating efficiently. Among these responsibilities are maintaining an inventory of supplies, overseeing the service contracts to keep the computers and fax machines running, and ordering new office equipment to support the professional staff.

Watching one secretary juggle all his or her jobs led one budget analyst to comment: "Within a week our secretary could do my job—I don't think I could do hers."

6

United States Park Police

The U.S. Park Police are the best-kept secret in the National Park Service. With only three field offices, in Washington, D.C., New York City, and San Francisco, this small force with an authorized strength of 655 police officers is unknown to most Park Service employees. Unless they work in the urban parks of the three cities, the average Park Service employees never come into contact with the U.S. Park Police.

The Park Police are unique. They are the only uniformed federal law-enforcement agency that performs duties similar to most city police officers. They mirror the metropolitan police of the three cities, providing the full range of police services. Their role is to furnish law-enforcement and protection services for visitors, resources, and facilities of National Park areas.

Historically, the Park Police predate both the Department of Interior (established in 1849) and the National Park Service (established in 1916). They trace their lineage back to 1791, when they were known as Park Watchmen. Initially, their jurisdiction extended only to the federally owned buildings and grounds within the nation's capital. In 1882, Congress gave the Park Watchmen concurrent jurisdiction with the D.C. Metropolitan Police Department and also granted the force the same authority and powers as the metro police. In 1948 their authority was again expanded to include

The Horsemounted Unit draws a crowd at an open house for drug education (U.S. Park Police).

federal areas in Virginia and Maryland within the environs of Washington.

The name was changed from Park Watchmen to United States Park Police in 1919. Until 1974, the Park Police operated only in the Washington area. In the early 1970s, Congress added two large urban parks to the National Park System: Gateway National Recreation Area in New York and New Jersey, and Golden Gate National Recreation Area in the San Francisco Bay area.

The policing of urban areas is basically foreign to the law enforcement ranger, and the rangers generally do not function as metropolitan police officers. Consequently, in 1974, the Park Police were directed to assume the law-enforcement responsibility for both Gateway and Golden Gate.

Although most of the force operates in the Washing-

United States Park Police

ton area, Park Police officers may be detailed to any part of the National Park System. Each regional office (except Alaska) has a Park Police captain serving as a law-enforcement specialist and instructor. These captains are responsible for coordinating law-enforcement and park ranger activities such as the protection of visiting heads of state. They also serve as instructors for the law enforcement rangers on topics ranging from crime prevention techniques to legal issues.

The Park Police protect certain federal facilities and resources, but like police everywhere, their primary duty is to protect lives. To accomplish this mission, they have developed specialized law-enforcement units to manage the diverse situations encountered in a large city.

The Horsemounted Unit, established in 1934, is one of the oldest and best-trained police equestrian units in the United States. Some sixty officers on horseback patrol the federal parks in the three cities. The unit participates in special events and demonstrations throughout the System. However, it is not just another traveling road show; it is a well-trained unit whose principal strength is crowd control.

All Park Police officers receive extensive crowd-control training, and the Horsemounted Unit provides additional support. Washington probably has more parades and demonstrations than any city or nation in the world. Demonstrations occur frequently in the city, which is the seat of the federal government. Groups like to march or protest in view of the monuments or the Capitol, since the possibility of national news coverage is greater.

Crowd control, therefore, can have ominous overtones. Marches can become obstructions. Demonstrations can become riots. Picket signs can become weapons. Both the officer and his or her mount must be prepared. As part of horsemounted training, the Park Police stage mock demonstrations of their own at the Rock Creek Park equestrian training facility in Washington. Utilizing recordings of crowd noise and simulating violent demonstrations, a team of horse and rider acquire the skills and build the confidence that have earned the unit the respect of their counterparts throughout the country. Park Police horses are trained to deal with the extremes of hostile crowds and too-friendly children. Horses are used to move and place people, not to attack them. The Park Police and their Horsemounted Unit have extensive experience in crowd-control techniques and often provide training for other law-enforcement agencies throughout the country.

Most demonstrations occur with only minor incidents; however, the demonstration protesting the visit of the Shah of Iran to President Carter in October 1977 was anything but minor. "We were preparing for a normal demonstration," Park Police Deputy Chief Jack Schamp describes. "We knew that the anti-Shah groups would be protesting, but we hadn't received any intelligence reports warning us about possible clashes between pro-Shah and anti-Shah groups.

"As President Carter was formally receiving the Shah on the back lawn of the White House, the two groups attacked each other with picket signs, rocks, and sticks. The anti-Shah protesters wore masks to avoid recognition and possible retaliation against their families back in Iran. Masked or not, we couldn't tell the 'good guys' from the 'bad guys', and we tried to get between the two groups. The protest became a riot. Our officers were attacked on both sides, and ninety-seven officers suffered injuries during the fighting." With so many officers hurt, the Park Police had to change tactics. "It was scary," recalls Jack. "We had to stop protecting the

UNITED STATES PARK POLICE

Park Police paramedic Gene Windsor rescues survivors of the Air Florida crash in the Potomac River (Charles Pereira photo, U.S. Park Police).

demonstrators from each other and start protecting ourselves. Our main concern was our fellow officers. Finally, we tear-gassed the rioters to disperse them. Unfortunately, some of the gas drifted to the welcoming ceremony at the White House, causing President Carter's eyes to tear."

Throughout the riot, the Horsemounted Unit performed magnificently. The horses never attacked the rioters, but instead attempted to block the opposing sides from each other and to protect the officers from stick-swinging fanatics.

The Park Police Aviation Unit has also received national acclaim. This unit is best known for its daring rescue of the survivors of the Air Florida Flight 90 crash in January 1982. Because of ice on its wings, the plane struggled on takeoff from Washington National Airport; never gaining altitude, it struck the 14th Street Bridge and plunged into the icy waters of the Potomac River. Severe weather conditions hampered rescue efforts as snow and sleet crippled traffic and clogged roadways. Surviving passengers clung desperately to pieces of wreckage.

Within minutes a Park Police helicopter arrived on the scene. While pilot Don Usher masterfully hovered the copter just feet above the water, paramedic Gene Windsor stood on the landing struts and grabbed survivors, clutching them while the pilot slowly flew toward shore to waiting rescue workers. Don and Gene performed this dangerous maneuver five times until the five surviving passengers were saved.

Currently, the helicopters in use are a Bell 206 Long Ranger and a Bell 412. The twin-engine Bell 412 provides added safety for the unit during their numerous river rescues and medevacs (emergency evacuation of sick or wounded) and has a seating capacity of fifteen, enough for an entire tactical team.

The Criminal Investigations Branch employs detectives and investigators who are responsible for investigating crimes committed on National Park Service property in the three cities. The branch consists of three sections: Major Crimes, Identification, and Special Investigations. The Major Crimes Section investigates all major crimes that come under the purview of the Park Police, from homicide, rape, and armed robbery to property crimes. The Identification Section assists the detectives in the forensic end of criminal investigations by gathering and processing evidence and recovering latent fingerprints. In the Special Investigations Section is the small but dynamic Narcotics/Vice Unit, which fights drug activity on Park Service lands.

The unit was created in 1983 on the recommendation of many of the street officers, to stem the increasing drug traffic in the Washington area parks. Working undercover much of the time, the officers concentrate on street-level drug dealing. "We target the source of the drugs and go after the dealers and distribution centers," explains Captain Charles Hume. "Of our 545 arrests in 1994, 406 were dealers. Taking down a drug network or removing the dealers is the only way to slow the traffic."

The Narcotics/Vice Unit requires special traits in its officers. "We're looking for aggressive officers with investigative ability who demonstrate an interest in narcotics enforcement and have distinguished themselves in some way," says Hume. "Drug dealers are extremely dangerous, and human life has no value to them. It takes tough men and women to accept the risks of undercover drug work."

Like other urban police forces, the Park Police have a Special Weapons and Assault Team (SWAT) Unit. The SWAT Unit and the Narcotics/Vice Unit combine their efforts in serving high-risk arrest and search warrants (sixty to eighty a year) in the Washington metropolitan area. The SWAT Unit is comprised of three six-officer teams. These highly trained teams are proficient with a variety of firearms, including the submachine gun, assault rifle, and sniper rifle, and they assume a leading role in barricade and hostage situations.

One day, I was in a meeting with Mrs. Mary Lou Grier, Deputy Director of the Park Service, to discuss increased funding for the wildfire management program. In the middle of the meeting, she was called away and never returned. We were frustrated, of course, but it was not until late that afternoon that we found out why she had left our meeting.

That morning, a man drove his van to the base of the Washington Monument. Claiming that his vehicle contained 1,000 pounds of dynamite, he vowed to detonate the explosives if his demands were not met. The Park Police SWAT teams surrounded the monument. The situation lasted for ten hours, and continual negotiation attempts failed. At 7:30 P.M., the man demonstrated his intention to drive into the downtown area and possibly detonate the explosives. Realizing that the loss of life and property would be far greater if he were allowed to leave the Monument grounds, the commander ordered the SWAT teams to stop him. As he tried to drive away from the Monument, he was shot by a SWAT marksman.

The Traffic Safety Unit does not receive the publicity or acclaim of the other units. Their job is traffic control and patrol of the park highways. They catch speeders and drunk drivers, untangle accidents, manage hazardous material spills, inspect tractor-trailers for safety and weight limitations, and do their best to protect us and keep the traffic flowing.

Through its Drug Recognition Expert program (DRE), the Traffic Safety Unit trains officers to recognize people who are under the influence of drugs and alcohol. A Driving While Intoxicated (DWI) program teaches the use and maintenance of breath-testing equipment. The Speed Enforcement Program certifies officers as radar operators and instructs them in the proper care of radar instruments. They use the latest enforcement equipment on the market, including a "radar detector-detector" to enforce the laws prohibiting radar detectors. They also use a laser speed detection instrument that is undetectable by radar operators and is target selective. The instrument enables the officer to pick out any vehicle in a pack and determine its speed.

UNITED STATES PARK POLICE

Motor Unit Officer Kelcy Stefansson, one of the first women motorcycle officers in federal law enforcement (U.S. Park Police).

When certain roadways are identified as problem areas with a high incidence of speeders or drunks, the Unit sets up a selective DWI and radar enforcement operation. After a few such crackdowns, the roadway gets a reputation as a place "crawling with cops," and driving improves for a short time—until it becomes necessary to reestablish the reputation.

Other Park Police units are the Canine Unit and the Motor Unit. The Canine Unit uses trained dogs to search for people and to detect drugs and explosives. The search and narcotics dogs are trained to discover drugs during searches of suspect houses and buildings. They also search for lost persons and "bailouts." A bailout is a person in a car chase who stops the car and runs away on foot. If the fugitive runs into the woods or out of sight of the chasing officer, the dogs are called to the scene. The dogs spend a minute or two in the fugitive's car getting the scent and then start tracking. They also find children who may have wandered away from a family picnic and gotten lost in the woods.

Bomb dogs are invaluable in sweeping and securing an area prior to the arrival of the President, Vice President, or a visiting head of state. These dogs work strictly on bomb detection. They are called into action for any bomb threat in the Washington area.

The Canine Unit receives its dogs by donation. There is room for eight dogs in the Unit. When donated, the dog lives with an officer and his family for a few weeks to see if they adjust to each other. If they hit it off, the dog becomes a member of the officer's family, living with them permanently while the dog and the officer go through at least three months of training. After training, the dog becomes part of the Canine Unit.

The Motor Unit uses motorcycles to perform traffic-control duties and serve in motorcades and as escorts for the President and other dignitaries. All visiting heads of state are either met at Andrews Air Force Base or helicoptered from Andrews to the Rainbow Pool, the official landing site at 17th and Independence Avenues, where the Motor Unit escorts them to their destination and provides escorts as needed during the visit.

The large motorcycles are highly visible during special events, demonstrations, and parades as the unit helps with crowd and traffic control. They have a fly-out team that travels anywhere a problem arises on federal lands. While the officers fly, the motorcycles and equipment are trucked to their destination. The team has traveled to Rocky Mountain National Park in Colorado and Zion National Park in Utah to quell unruly motorcycle gangs. They have also traveled to Miami and Fort Chaffee, Arkansas, to help control large numbers of Cuban boatpeople who travel to the States. Because of their experience in a variety of urban situations, the Motor Unit often conducts motorcycle training classes for other federal, state, and local law-enforcement agencies.

Another unit of the Park Police is the uniformed guard force that protects federal property and buildings. Guards either serve at fixed posts or patrol assigned areas to prevent theft, trespass, fire, or vandalism. Most guards are permanent, part-time employees located in the National Capital Region, the Washington area. A few are based in other regions, and some have full-time positions. Irregular hours are common, because the guards usually work through the night.

Despite the irregular hours and exposure to hazardous and stressful situations, intense competition prevails for positions with the Park Police. Applicants must pass a written test. All applicants must be twenty-one but under thirty-one years of age, have a high school diploma or equivalent, and have either two years of progressively responsible experience or two years of college. They must possess good vision (20/100 or better that is correctable to 20/20 with glasses or contact lenses), pass a physical and medical examination prior to final selection, and undergo a personal background investigation.

Although the competition is tough, many Force members are approaching retirement eligibility, and more openings should be available soon. Rookie officers go to the Federal Law Enforcement Training Center (FLETC) at Glynco, Georgia, for eighteen weeks of police training. After FLETC come eleven weeks of the Field Training Officer Program, in which rookies are assigned to a veteran officer to learn street smarts and develop common-sense approaches to various situations. "I believe it takes a year to make a cop," says Deputy Chief Jack Schamp. "The training never stops. We continue specialized training such as profiling." Certain types of cars tend to be ripped off by certain age groups. When an officer observes erratic driving or joyriding by people and cars that match a profile, he radios in for stolen-car information and a license check. "We stop a lot of stolen cars through profiling," explains Jack. As new equipment surfaces or new techniques develop, the Park Police officers receive training to apply the innovations and compile evidence. "Solid evidence is essential in court cases, and we don't want a case thrown out or a conviction overturned because we didn't train our people properly."

The Park Police have a recruiting brochure for interested applicants. For information, write to: U.S. Park Police, Personnel Section, 1100 Ohio Drive SW, Washington, DC 20242; or phone: (202) 619-7056.

If you are appointed, you will join a small but elite police force tasked with a difficult but rewarding job. As I watched the Washington Redskins victory parade through downtown Washington after the 1992 Super

Bowl, the Park Police Horsemounted Unit expertly cleared a path through the crowd for the team to exit the buses and stand on the speaker's podium. Anchorman Jim Vance of WRC-TV narrated the parade for the television audience. As he identified the Park Police, he admiringly told the audience, "No one has more experience working with crowds. These guys know what they are doing!" Jim Vance's words are a testament to the entire force of the U.S. Park Police.

7

Maintenance Workers

Mention maintenance workers, and the typical response is: "Oh, yeah. The guys who pick up the trash and clean the toilets." Unfortunately, that response is the public's image of a Park Service maintenance worker. Yes, the maintenance people do haul trash and clean toilets, but they also keep the park functioning in ways that the public never considers.

Maintenance work for 368 park units encompassing 83 million acres of land takes a big portion of the annual Park Service operating budget, approximately $347 million in 1995. Visitors come to the parks with certain expectations. They may expect to see wild animals or breathtaking scenery, or to listen to a campfire talk by an interpretive ranger. The one constant expectation they bring is the clean, attractive setting that greets them upon entering the park.

The Park Service has a maintenance responsibility for every asset they own, and they take that responsibility seriously. You won't see hit-or-miss work when you explore a park. You may see a road crew patching potholes, a trail crew removing downed trees from a hiking trail, or a carpenter replacing a stairway in a historic building. The carpenter won't just be building a new stairway. He'll be restoring the stairway exactly as it was constructed, using the same cuts and joints as the original.

Each park has a maintenance division. The larger the park, the more people are needed. The small parks can get by with a few maintenance workers or even one or two "jack-of-all-trades" types who are invaluable anywhere but essential in a small park. Most of the maintenance workers in any park are local people who have lived in the area most of their lives and expect to stay. In contrast, the park rangers are mobile and routinely move from park to park as their career progresses. Historically, very little movement occurred in the maintenance ranks except among the top jobs, the facility manager (chief of maintenance) position in each park. Today, however, maintenance workers are becoming more mobile and advancing up the career ladder by following the "move out, move up" philosophy.

The management of maintenance work has changed drastically in the last ten years. Computers have changed the way work is organized and planned. Facility managers have been forced to change and become computer literate.

The Park Service has implemented a computerized Maintenance Management (MM) program, enabling facility managers to plan, organize, direct, and control their maintenance work. Under MM, all national parks follow the same guidelines; however, each park may customize parts of the program to meet local needs. The program furnishes information on how long it takes to mow an acre of grounds, paint 100 square feet of surface, or plow a mile of road, and it provides a cost-per-unit measure. This type of information allows the manager to build a budget for the year and factor in scenarios to anticipate budget cuts or budget increases. The program generates performance reports comparing the work planned with the work accomplished.

The facility manager uses the information in the program to build biweekly schedules at the beginning of the

Maintenance Workers

Laying the foundation for a sidewalk at St. Croix National Scenic Riverway (National Park Service).

year. This way, employees know their schedule for a two-week period. The MM program is much more complicated than this short overview suggests, but it enables facility managers to know how much time and money each activity requires and where they can improve their operation.

Let's look at some of the work that maintenance people do. Shenandoah National Park in Virginia, popular with residents of the Washington, D.C. area, is a long, narrow park lying along an 80-mile stretch of the Blue Ridge Mountains. This unique configuration presents special problems to the maintenance division. "On any summer evening, 4,000 people are staying overnight in the park," says Rodney Lowe, facility manager for twenty-five years. "Providing services at Shenandoah is similar to maintaining a small city. The difference is that a city may have one water supply and sewer system, while the park has thirty. We service everything from modern waste-water treatment facilities to septic tanks."

Lowe has a staff of 100 people and an annual budget of some $4 million to maintain the park. Shenandoah's visitor season is March to Thanksgiving. Some parks hire seasonal help during their visitor season, but Shenandoah's workers are all permanent employees. The difference is that fifty-five employees work year-round while the other forty-five are classified as "permanent but subject to furlough." These forty-five are laid off for three to four months during the off-season, but their health and insurance benefits continue during their furlough.

The maintenance division has three responsibilities in a park:

1. Daily operations: Pick up garbage and haul it to the landfill, clean and restock the restrooms, pick up litter, clean the campgrounds, mow lawns, and ensure that the roads are clear.
2. Maintenance of park facilities and equipment: This is where the true maintenance aspect comes into play, as buildings and equipment are repaired, broken systems (water lines, sewer systems) are fixed, and the park is kept running. Shenandoah's mechanics have over 200 pieces of moving equipment (cars, trucks, bulldozers, etc.) and 300 pieces of motor-driven equipment (chain saws, lawn mowers, weed whackers, etc.) to keep running. If equipment breaks, work stops. Building maintenance workers not only keep historic buildings safe and weathertight, but are also preservationists, sensitive to the historic fabric of the building and traditional construction methods.

Maintenance Workers

3. Construction: Most large parks have workers skilled in the construction trades who build buildings and roads. This is the most satisfying aspect of the job for maintenance workers because they can look at the finished product, be it a ranger station, picnic pavilion, or two miles of road, and be proud as they witness the proof of their labors.

These three responsibilities require diverse skills in a maintenance crew: landscape architects, engineers, laborers, heavy equipment operators, and craftsmen. Among the craftsmen employed at Shenandoah are carpenters, sign makers, plumbers, painters, electricians, waste-water plant operators, and mechanics.

Most maintenance divisions have two main branches, Buildings and Utilities (B&U) and Roads and Trails (R&T). The professionals, who are landscape arthitects and engineers, are paid on the GS scale or the WS (wage manager may be paid on the GS scale or the WS (wage supervisor) scale. The laborers and craftsmen are on the WG (wage grade) scale. (See Appendix 3 for an explanation of grade scales.)

The career ladder for a worker in the B&U Branch would typically go like this: A laborer is hired at the WG-3 level, progresses to a WG-5 assisting one of the craftsmen, then goes to a WG-7 level, such as a plumber or carpenter worker. The next stop is the journeyman level, WG-9/10, and from there to foreman. In the WG positions, workers can compete for any opening if they can do the job. If qualified, a person can jump from a laborer to a craftsman position. Skilled workers often take the first open position just to get a job with the Park Service, and then compete for higher positions as they open.

In the Roads and Trails branch, the laborer, WG-3,

Maintenance worker Alphonso Promutico operates an alcohol-fueled lawn mower on the National Mall (National Park Service).

moves to a WG-5/7 as a motor vehicle operator driving dump trucks, garbage compactors, low-boys, and snowplows. The next level is engineering equipment operator, WG-8/10, driving bulldozers, backhoes, front-end loaders, or road graders. From moving equipment, a person can advance to foreman.

A foreman is eligible to become a facility manager, one of the division chiefs on a superintendent's staff and part of the management team. The facility manager receives the park maintenance priorities from the superintendent and plans the work within the money allocated to the division. He runs the everyday maintenance operations and oversees the workforce, organizing the work crews with his foremen.

One of the most important programs that management can provide to an employee is training opportuni-

Maintenance Workers

ties. In 1988 the Park Service created an employee development training program for maintenance foremen. Workers advance to foreman positions after proving themselves excellent craftsmen. As their responsibilities grow, they may encounter difficulties created by general administration demands (like paperwork), personnel management, budgeting, and multi-year planning.

The seven-week training program at the Albright Training Center in Grand Canyon National Park is designed to qualify the foreman for a position as a facility manager throughout the Park Service. After the course, trainees spend an additional four weeks in a park working with a facility manager to gain practical experience.

"We need people whose career goal is to be a facility manager in a park," says Ted Hillmer, regional chief of maintenance for the Midwest Region in Omaha, Nebraska. He is an advocate for training maintenance people to become managers. "I want to see maintenance people attain the same professional status as the ranger and be able to compete for superintendent positions."

The superintendent position has traditionally been the duty of the ranger, but that is changing. Sue McGill worked her way through maintenance positions, from motor vehicle operator at Carlsbad Caverns National Park in New Mexico to Buildings and Utilities foreman. She then transferred to facility manager positions at the USS *Arizona* Memorial in Hawaii and Bryce Canyon National Park in Utah before assuming her current position as superintendent at Timpanogos Cave National Monument in Utah. Frustrated by her slow progress through the ranger ranks, Sue switched to the maintenance field because she saw more opportunity to advance.

Installing riprap (boulders/broken concrete) along the shoreline to prevent erosion at Sleeping Bear Dunes National Lakeshore (National Park Service).

More people with degrees in architecture, engineering, and landscape architecture are moving into maintenance careers. "Combine education with training and experience, and there's no reason a maintenance person shouldn't have the opportunity to be a superintendent," says Hillmer.

Maintenance workers definitely have a wealth of experience in park operations. They are involved in some way with every division of a park. They work regularly with natural resource managers to stabilize trails from erosion and combat exotic plants intruding on the park's native vegetation. Cultural resource managers are consulted about repairs to historic buildings. Maintenance workers design and build trail systems for interpreters and work with historians in removing hazardous trees in a historic area to minimize the impact on the setting. If excavation is needed, they work with archeologists. In the course of their work, they have to negotiate the tangle of federal and state environmental guidelines. For this reason, maintenance divisions consult with the environmental compliance person, who guides the crews on environmentally safe methods of performing their jobs. The compliance specialist is knowledgeable about the federal and state environmental laws and Environmental Protection Agency regulations, including which chemical herbicides and pesticides are approved for use in the parks.

With visitation increasing in the national parks, maintenance is forced to work harder and do more with the same amount of money. Innovative facility managers are using volunteers to supplement their maintenance crews. Many facility managers involve the local community in maintaining the park. Boy Scouts and other groups pitch in on trail and road cleanups.

For almost twenty years, Shenandoah has operated a Youth Conservation Corps (YCC) program employing twenty-four teenagers and their leaders. Rodney Lowe puts them to work on labor-intensive projects such as rebuilding water and sewer lines, to take advantage of their youthful energy. Shenandoah also receives assistance from hiking clubs in the Washington area. The Appalachian Trail runs through the park, and the trail clubs work with the park to clean and maintain this world-famous trail.

In an effort to attract college students to a maintenance career with the Park Service, Ted Hillmer expanded a summer seasonal program in the Midwest Region for junior and senior college students studying architecture, engineering, or landscape architecture. The students work in the regional office and in the parks. They are given specific projects, such as designing a building addition or a walkway through a marsh. They are paid at the GS-4 level, about $8.35 per hour. The park benefits from their work, and the students gain professional job experience. The program also opens their eyes to possible employment with the Park Service. Most students in these disciplines don't realize that the Park Service has a need for their skills. For information about this program, write to: National Park Service, Midwest Regional Office, 1709 Jackson Street, Omaha, NE 68102-2571.

8

Backcountry Rangers

If you want to know what ranger work used to be like in the early days of the Park Service, become a backcountry ranger. Before creation of the National Park Service in 1916, the U.S. Cavalry patrolled and protected the fourteen national parks and twenty-one national monuments in existence at the time. Upon establishment of the Service, many of the scouts and cavalrymen left the Army to form the core of the first ranger force. Accustomed to living in the open, depending on their own ingenuity and survival skills, these men and their stories provide fond memories of being a ranger in the days when the West was still wild.

The backcountry rangers are the closest link with this past, as they emulate the rugged independence of their predecessors. Patrolling wilderness trails for eight days at a stretch with only your horse for company; standing atop a mountain and watching the sun come up to announce a new day; spending days in some of America's most beautiful wilderness settings—these are just some situations of the backcountry ranger.

To be a backcountry ranger you have to pay a price, but it's a price many are willing to pay. Living conditions are primitive at best. Dave Shea, a professor at Southwestern Oregon Community College in Coos Bay, spent fourteen years as a seasonal backcountry ranger in Glacier National Park, Montana. Dave patrolled the Belly River area in the northeast corner—roadless country encompassing 100 square miles of true wilderness, stretching from prairie grasslands on the north to the Continental Divide on the south.

Dave and his wife, Genevieve, lived in a log ranger station constructed in 1925. That doesn't sound so bad. Actually, it projects a cozy and idyllic image until you consider that the station was six miles from the nearest road and had no electricity. Contact with the outside world was by radio. They had inside plumbing, which Dave connected and disconnected every spring and fall. A propane refrigerator, wood cooking stove, and a cooler built in a nearby creek completed their luxuries. They would arrive in late April, often hiking through snow, and depart in early October. Company arrived in June when another backcountry ranger, a fire guard, and a four-man trail crew took up residence in a nearby cabin and two large tent frames.

Brian Chan has life a bit easier. Brian is the full-time backcountry supervisor for the Lamar subdistrict in the northeast corner of Yellowstone National Park. He lives year-round in the frontcountry (near civilization) in a cabin at the Lamar Ranger Station, about an hour's drive from the Montana towns of Gardiner and West Yellowstone and 25 miles from Cooke City. From this base, Brian and one seasonal ranger patrol 275,000 acres of backcountry, 106 miles of trail, and 33 campsites.

Backcountry rangers have a variety of responsibilities. They patrol the trails and protect the safety of travelers. They do trail maintenance work, placing water bars along trails and often using chain saws to clear downed trees. Water bars are 6-inch-diameter lengths of wood that are put in the ground at angles along a trail to divert water and prevent erosion. During heavy rains, water normally follows a trail, digging gullies in it.

Trail crews from the maintenance division normally maintain the trails, but the size of the parks precludes their doing it all. The maintenance division prioritizes their work and does what it can, but needs the backcountry rangers to help out.

On the patrols, the rangers clean messy campsites and fire rings to extinguish any flickering embers. But most important is their contact with the backcountry travelers: hikers and campers.

Anyone going into the backcountry needs a permit, which is available free of charge from the visitor centers and ranger stations. Backcountry travelers must use designated campsites, which can be reserved no more than forty-eight hours in advance. As part of the permit, visitors list their proposed itinerary with the rangers. They are encouraged to tell friends of their trip and ask the friends to notify the park if they haven't checked in by a specified date. If a party is reported overdue, rangers immediately start search and rescue operations, using the itinerary to define the search area.

Yellowstone has a backcountry office at park headquarters in Mammoth Hot Springs, where permits from the entire park are logged. This office has all the current information on trail conditions and campsite availability. The backcountry rangers radio this office with reports of washed-out trails or closed campsites. The backcountry office also lets Brian know how many people are in his area.

The rangers who issue permits tell travelers about park regulations and give guidelines on minimum-impact camping and bear encounters. The backcountry rangers meeting travelers on the trail subtly continue to educate them about how to camp without disturbing the natural surroundings. Many campers still believe that if you need firewood, you chop down the nearest tree. Rangers instruct them to gather wood from downed, dead trees.

Brian considers meeting and talking to backcountry travelers one of the most important aspects of his job. "After a few days alone, it's nice to talk to someone," he remarks. "I like to talk about the park and some of the history of the Lamar area, point out some good places to hike and fish. The visitors seem to enjoy it, too."

And then there are the bears. "I spend a lot of time answering questions about grizzlies. I'll spend as much time as they want if it means saving someone from injury or death and preventing a bear from being destroyed." Brian tells them to hang their food ten feet off the ground and four feet away from another tree. He has installed food poles for this purpose in most of the campsites. Campers are instructed to cook in the fire rings, or near the food pole at campsites where fires aren't permitted, and to eat all food in the cooking area. "Try to keep all the food odors in one area," he emphasizes. "Don't walk around camp eating and spreading food odors." Once the cooking area is cleaned (be sure to wash the dishes) and the food is hung, camp at least 100 yards from the cooking area. If the bears can't get at the food, they are more likely to get discouraged and leave.

In Yosemite National Park, California, the number of incidents between black bears and humans resulting in property damage and, to a lesser extent, injury remained at a constant level despite efforts to educate backcountry users. To combat this problem the superintendent initiated a unique interpretive program. Five wilderness interpreters began traveling Yosemite's backcountry to educate hikers and campers about black bear behavior, proper food storage, and the park's management of the bear population. They spend five days a week in the backcountry, hiking to locations popular

BACKCOUNTRY RANGERS

Ranger Brian Chan with horses packed for an eight-day trip into Yellowstone's backcountry (Lynn Bickerton photo).

with overnight visitors and with bears, to spread their message.

Many experienced backcountry travelers respectfully share the bear's environment and feel fortunate to actually see one, but in truth most people are terrified of encountering a bear. Dave Shea recalls the time he returned late to the ranger station after an all-day horseback patrol to find four hikers huddled on his front porch. "They had been there most of the day because they could hear a wounded grizzly bawling in the distance," remembers Dave. "I led them a short distance to the corral, where they saw the 'wounded grizzly.' It was my mule, braying away, venting displeasure at being left behind in the pasture all day."

Besides educating the public and protecting them from wildlife, backcountry rangers have to protect the wildlife from poachers. Yellowstone is a haven for elk, buffalo, moose, and grizzlies. Some animals are killed by poachers seeking a trophy; others are slaughtered indiscriminately for their antlers and body parts. The rangers have law-enforcement commissions, carry firearms on patrol, and can make arrests. Rangers are constantly on watch for poaching activity and report by radio to headquarters if they encounter evidence of it.

Rangers routinely check permits to see where travelers are heading and pass on trail and campsite information. "I check the time of day against their schedule to see if they can make their campsite on time," says Brian. "If they are behind schedule, I can suggest closer campsites that I know are available." Travelers without permits are liable to receive a citation. Other offenses meriting a citation include traveling with a pet, carrying a firearm, camping or building a fire in undesignated areas, littering, and fishing violations.

During his patrols, Brain may be out for eight to ten days, and he plans his travels to stay each night at one of the five cabins in the Lamar backcountry. Each trip includes pack animals loaded with food, camping equipment, and Coleman fuel to restock the cabins. Camping equipment is necessary for the cold nights spent outside when the cabin is too far, and Coleman fuel keeps the lanterns glowing. The cabins are kept supplied with food and fuel. Major restocking is done before winter in case the cabin is needed for search and rescue operations.

According to Dave, "All of our gear, supplies, and groceries come in and out on pack animals. A good knowledge of packing supplies and handling stock is essential." Dave had plenty of practice. He would radio out a food order every few weeks, and it would be delivered to the trailhead, six miles from his cabin. He would take the horses and mule and pack it back to the ranger station. "We supplemented our supplies with a small garden plot near the cabin. The plot provided a great deal of our food, but more important, it was fresh food." Brain also appreciates fresh food. "I always start out with fresh food that I eat for the first few days," he says. "Try eating canned food for four or five days. It gets old real quick."

Backcountry rangers also engage in resource management activities. Their knowledge of the area and its wildlife and vegetation sensitizes them to any changes. "We have our fingers on the pulse of the backcountry," Brain remarks. "When changes in exotic plant growth or numbers of wildlife are observed, we work with the resource manager to stop any damage." He is currently participating in a study to monitor campground impacts at sites where horses and grazing are allowed. By running transects and measuring vegetation production, the resource managers can determine whether the campsite area is healthy or declining and in need of a rest.

Dave monitored Glacier's wildlife and their movements. Because of his special interest in wildlife and botany, he kept extensive records of daily and seasonal animal sightings and a list of plant species, which he shared with the resource management staff. "There were good populations of all kinds of wildlife including grizzlies, elk, and even an occasional wolf," Dave remembers. "Well over 100 bird species occur in the Belly River area, including nesting golden eagles, prairie falcons, and loons."

Dave's crew spent time fighting forest fires at least once a year. Each day the fire guard recorded the weather conditions from instruments at the ranger station and radioed the readings to the park fire office.

A major concern for the rangers is hazardous trail conditions, which are the main reason for backcountry patrols. Hazardous trail conditions place unsuspecting visitors at risk. The hazards take many forms. Bear activity along a trail or campsite could cause the rangers to close the area until the bears move on. Particularly dangerous is an animal carcass on a trail. A dead elk on or near a trail is a magnet. If the bears have not discovered the carcass, the rangers remove it. If the bears have begun feeding on it, however, they give it a wide berth and close the trail and campsites in the area, rerouting visitors and allowing the bears to feed undisturbed.

Backcountry travelers are aware of the danger of surprising a sow bear with cubs, but just as perilous is stumbling upon a bear's food cache. Brian has found an elk carcass buried by a bear near a campsite and immediately closed the area and radioed the closure to the park backcountry office.

Other visitor hazards are tree snags that can fall without warning. They are especially prevalent in the burned areas of Yellowstone. Maintenance crews have removed the most dangerous and visible ones along the trails, but snags still exist away from the trails. Rangers advise travelers to stay on the trail in burned areas and be cautious in strong winds.

In the event of injury to a visitor in the backcountry, the rangers have a certain degree of emergency medical training to help the injured person until a rescue team arrives. Beginning with CPR and ending with paramedics, the Park Service has seven levels of emergency medical training to support their policy that "the saving of human life takes precedence over all other park management activities."

There is too much work in the backcountry for the rangers and trail crews to accomplish, so help arrives in the form of the Youth Conservation Corps (YCC) and the Student Conservation Association (SCA). These volunteer organizations are active in national parks

Backcountry Rangers

throughout the country and complete valuable projects at no cost to the park. They typically work on labor-intensive projects such as trail construction or rehabilitation. The backcountry rangers set up a schedule of projects they want accomplished during the season. Some projects, such as installing food poles at campsites, are completed in stages during their patrols. Other projects require help from the YCC or SCA. Usually these groups camp in the backcountry for long stretches, and the rangers load the packhorses and haul supplies to them.

Some of the projects include maintenance and upkeep of the ranger station and backcountry cabins. Each cabin has a logbook, and the rangers record their observations along the trail and what work they have done to the cabin. As a general rule, backcountry rangers keep a personal log of their activities, wildlife reports, special occurrences, and an annual summary report. These logs are often on file at the ranger station and park headquarters.

Come October, or earlier if the weather turns cold, Dave and Genevieve load their packhorses and return to civilization in Oregon. Brian, however, is a full-time backcountry ranger, and he doesn't get a break come winter. There are two trails in his subdistrict that are used by cross-country skiers. Donning his skis, Brian patrols and maintains the trails. Back at his ranger station home, he plans the projects for the next year and catches up with the less glorious administrative aspects of the job.

Both men relish their life in the outdoors and their independence. Dave expresses it best, "The joy of living in and protecting such a beautiful wilderness, the abundant wildlife and natural wonders, and the pleasure of meeting people on the trail make this a rare and extremely rewarding job."

9

Park Planners

Have you ever wondered how a national park comes into existence? Did you think that the Park Service just goes out and claims a scenic or historic area as a national park? It's not that easy. Congress, your elected Senators and Representatives, determines whether or not an area becomes part of the National Park System. Congress passes a law designating a national park. The law, known as the enabling legislation, defines the purpose of the park and includes various specifications as to size and boundaries, land acquisition limits, and management guidelines.

For example, in 1978 Congress passed P.L. 95-625, known as the National Parks and Recreation Act of 1978. This act designated a number of parks, wild and scenic rivers, and national trails as new units of the National Park System. The P.L. stands for Public Law; the 95 means 95th Congress. The 625 is the number of laws the 95th Congress had passed at that point in time.

How does this relate to park planners? Planners usually get into the act before and after an area is designated as a national park. Congress passes legislation, such as P.L. 95-625, directing the Park Service to study specific areas for possible inclusion in the National Park System and report its findings. These are called new area studies, and the study period is usually from a few months to three years. If the report recommends the area for designation, Congress may or may not act upon it. A negative report usually eliminates the area from further consideration.

For existing or newly designated parks, the Park Service is required to develop a plan known as a General Management Plan (GMP). A GMP outlines the basic management philosophy for a park and provides strategies for achieving the management objectives over a fifteen-year period.

Planning is different for each new area to determine its eligibility for the National Park System. The planning team determines whether the new area has significant or unique resources on a national, regional, state, or local level. If the resources are nationally significant, the area must also meet criteria for suitability and feasibility to qualify as a potential addition.

I was part of numerous study teams when I worked on the Wild and Scenic Rivers Program and the National Trails Program in the early 1980s. Through legislation, Congress gave the Park Service a list of rivers and trails to study for possible inclusion in the two Systems. The study teams usually consist of six to eight members from the Washington and regional office. These teams are called interdisciplinary because they are composed of specialists with varying backgrounds and expertise. A typical team has specialists in natural resources, real estate appraisal, recreational planning, cultural resources, and interpretation. Other members are brought aboard as needed. Landscape architects, engineers, historians, and social scientists often serve on planning teams.

The first step in the study is a reconnaissance survey, which is a fact-finding effort only. The team holds one or more public meetings to explain why they are in the area and what they will be doing. These meetings can be very helpful. The residents give valuable information about the history of the area. They can also be hostile. I've participated in a number of meetings at which the residents believed we were there to select their land for federal ownership and would just as soon hang us as not.

During the survey, team members fan out and gather information. The completed report discusses the area's natural, scenic, and cultural resources. The recreation values are assessed. Is it a unique area for recreation or is it typical of the region? An important part of the report is land ownership, including existing and proposed land uses. Are commercial developments under way or planned that would harm the area's resources? Have the current land uses such as farming, mining, or residential development hurt the significance of the area? Are the existing resources protected by any local or state provisions?

If the team finds that the area is not nationally significant, the study is usually concluded. If it is determined to be nationally significant, a further study, known as a study of alternatives report, is done to examine the best ways to protect and manage the area.

The alternatives report elaborates upon the survey report but also examines various feasible alternatives for the management, protection, and use of the area. Each alternative is analyzed for its economic, social, cultural, and environmental impact.

To give you an idea of management alternatives, let's consider the four alternatives in a fictional study of the Great Dismal Swamp in Virginia and North Carolina:

Alternative 1: Establish Great Dismal Swamp National Park in Virginia and North Carolina, to be managed by the National Park Service.

Alternative 2: Establish Great Dismal Swamp National Wildlife Refuge in Virginia, to be managed by the U.S. Fish and Wildlife Service.

Alternative 3: No action. (This is a required alternative in each study and discusses the predicted scenario for the area without protection.)

Alternative 4: Virginia and North Carolina should establish state parks at Great Dismal Swamp.

The list of alternatives can be long or short depending on the feasible concepts for an area, but the above list should give you an idea of the process. After closely analyzing all available information, the team recommends one alternative.

If the recommended alternative finds that the area should be added to the National Park System, the Secretary of the Interior transmits the report to Congress with that recommendation and with a legislative data package containing estimates of any necessary funding. The package may also contain draft legislation. In these times of budget deficits and federal program cutbacks, the cost estimates of a new park take on added importance.

Now let's look at the General Management Plans that guide a park's management and development. The plans set a course of action for fifteen years and are updated periodically, giving the superintendent a blueprint for running the park. Superintendents work closely with the GMP team.

The planning teams also are interdisciplinary. Members should have expertise in park planning, natural or cultural resources, concessions management, environmental design, and interpretation. This core team is supplemented as needed by specialists in geology, forestry, wildlife management, economics, transportation,

Park Planners

energy conservation, air and water quality, engineering, and law.

Planners present two types of strategies in a GMP: those required to manage the park's resources and those required to provide for visitor use and interpretation of the resources. Based on these strategies, any development deemed necessary for operation of the parks is identified. The GMP also identifies the environmental impacts of the developments and the park operations.

GMPs can become quite detailed. Basically, the park is categorized by four zones: natural, historic, park development, and special use. These zones indicate the management emphasis and the type of development appropriate for each.

The management emphasis in the natural zone is on conserving resources, interpreting unique ecological or geological features for the public, providing environmentally compatible recreation activities, and setting aside certain areas for strict protection because of their unusual fragility or ecological significance. Facilities in the natural zone include foot trails, signs and trailside information displays, small boat docks, and primitive shelters for hikers.

The emphasis in the historic zone is on preserving, protecting, and interpreting historic sites, structures, and objects associated with people or events in human history. There is little development in historic zones; usually interpretive displays and markers.

The park development zone is the area developed to serve the needs of park management and visitors. Developments include visitor centers, administrative headquarters, ranger stations, maintenance yards, campgrounds, marinas, restaurants, hotels, gas stations, and park housing. Such developments substantially alter the natural environment or the setting of historically significant resources. The idea is to concentrate them in a small part of the park.

Special use zones are areas over which the Park Service does not have full control. Other government agencies or private interests have prior control over land use within the park. Such activities include timber-cutting, mining and drilling, ranching, farming, and private housing. The park tries to work with these interests to minimize any impact on the park resources.

Besides delineating the four management zones, the GMP examines and makes recommendations on the status of natural and cultural resources, the needs of the interpretive program, and the types and extent of the concessions required for visitors. The plan also discusses possible boundary adjustments and land protection ideas. In the special use zones, when a park contains nonfederal lands, strategies need to be developed to assure that the special uses are consistent with the park purpose.

Plans, no matter how detailed, are useless if they are not implemented. The GMP contains a phased sequence of actions to be taken and the estimated costs.

This is an abbreviated version of park planning. Planning can be an immensely rewarding occupation; however, it is a long-range activity, and years may elapse before your work comes to fruition. Area study plans that I worked on in the 1980s periodically rise from the dead, only to be snuffed out by lack of Congressional support. On the other hand, river studies that I helped prepare were acted upon, and some rivers became part of the National Wild and Scenic Rivers System. It is a tremendous satisfaction to realize that your work was instrumental in saving a river from being dammed and having it preserved and protected by the National Park Service.

10

Architects, Engineers, and Landscape Architects

When you think of the Park Service, the ranger immediately springs to mind as the symbol of the organization. But the rangers comprise only 24 percent of the total workforce. Some of the most anonymous employees are those who design and direct the construction of the visitor centers, campgrounds, roads, and other park buildings and facilities. The Park Service employs many architects, engineers, and landscape architects.

The majority are employed at the Denver Service Center in Lakewood, Colorado. The Service Center does the major planning, design, and construction work for the entire Park Service. The 700-member professional office is the Park Service equivalent of a large architectural/engineering (A/E) firm. Their work is broader in scope, however, because they design and construct facilities that must blend in with the park environment and be faithful to the mission of protecting the resources. On the Service Center staff are architects, historians, planners, landscape architects, and many kinds of engineers.

Projects of significant cost are prepared by the Service Center. Smaller projects may be completed in the regional offices, which usually have a small engineering and architecture staff, or the region may contract with a private A/E firm. The actual design of a project is so time-consuming that the regional offices contract out about 75 to 80 percent of their work to private firms. Even the Service Center often has an overwhelming workload and uses private firms, but it oversees this contracted work.

Architects develop the concept for a structure, and the engineers figure out how to make it work. How should it look? What is its function? Where should it be placed to blend in with the natural surroundings? What materials should be used? Will the soil conditions support the structure? What are the maintenance requirements? Will the visual impact of the structure affect the natural or historic scene? Where will utilities come from?

Architects, engineers, and landscape architects consider these and other questions when they design a structure. After the initial ideas are discussed and accepted by the park and the regional office, the architects and engineers develop construction contract documents that show the structure's appearance, details of its construction, and cost estimates. These documents often take two years to complete because they include drawings of the structural system, air conditioning, heating, ventilating, plumbing, and electrical systems. Projects along the West Coast, particularly in California and Alaska, have to be designed to withstand earthquakes.

Landscape architects provide the plans for the outside of the structure. In developing a design, architects must follow building and fire codes and provide easy access for handicapped persons. Civil engineers design roads, tunnels, bridges, and water and sewer systems.

When the construction contract documents are complete, the project is contracted out to a private construc-

Architects, Engineers, and Landscape Architects

tion company by competitive bidding. A Service Center engineer stays on site to oversee the construction.

The Service Center has three teams, East, West, and Central. Each team is divided into three branches, planning, design, and construction. The planning branch works with the superintendent to produce the GMP and other plans that guide the development of the park. The design branch completes the designs and construction contract documents. The construction branch assigns a construction supervisor, also known as contracting officer representative (COR), to ensure that the contractor complies with all specifications.

The teams also rehabilitate historic buildings and the infrastructure of existing buildings. They also work on projects to remove existing structures from prime resource areas. In Sequoia National Park, California, some of the early buildings were placed without regard to their impact on the park's resources, particularly the sequoia trees. The buildings and the accompanying traffic killed some of the older sequoias and inhibited the regeneration of others. Replacement facilities are planned in a less sensitive area about five miles away.

Architects, engineers, and landscape architects are also employed in the regional offices and in the larger parks. In the parks, they frequently work in the maintenance division, often as facility manager (chief of maintenance).

Brad Traver, the park engineer at Grand Canyon National Park, Arizona, works for the superintendent. His job does not entail as much actual engineering as it does managing design and construction work. He advises the superintendent on the feasibility of planned park projects and oversees the work by the Service Center or a private A/E firm.

Currently he is reviewing the designs for a large employee housing project, two park roads, and a road under construction. He is also overseeing a lead-abatement program to remove lead paint in the park. He wrote a detailed scope-of-work report identifying the necessary steps and estimating the cost for this project. The regional office uses his scope-of-work report to write a contract for the work.

Landscape architects plan the location of buildings, roads, and walkways, as well as the arrangement of native shrubs and trees. They work with architects and engineers to determine the best layout of roads and buildings.

Bob Elmore worked both as a park planner at Indiana Dunes National Lakeshore in Indiana and as the park landscape architect at Mount Rainier National Park in Washington. To plan new developments in these parks, he had to first analyze site plans which take into account existing topography, vegetation, roads, trails, building locations, and local environmental conditions. He then reviewed proposed projects from the Service Center. His assignments involved protecting natural sites by rerouting roads or trails away from the sites. Sometimes he had to protect a natural site but still provide access for visitors. At Indiana Dunes, trails were designed and built that allowed the visitor to see and enjoy the fragile dunes without damaging them.

Besides new development, Bob also created landscape plans for sites such as campgrounds, scenic vistas, picnic areas, roadside pull-offs, and buildings in the park development zone.

Landscape architects have to both deal with wide ranges of climate and topography and utilize native trees and shrubs that blend with the vegetation at the site. At Mount Rainier, Bob worked in a park with 378 square miles between elevations of 2,000 feet and 14,410 feet above sea level. Climate ranges varied from

Architects, Engineers, and Landscape Architects

the moist forests of Douglas fir to arctic conditions at the higher elevations. Facilities had to be designed to function year–round—even in rain and heavy snow—and accommodate over two million visitors per year.

At historical sites, research is required to capture a picture of the scene at the time the historical event occurred at that spot. Then the landscape architect tries to duplicate the exact scene. For all the site projects, the landscape architect prepares cost estimates and may be the COR for contracted work.

For parks without an engineer or landscape architect, the work is performed by the regional office or one of the Denver Service Center teams. One of the attractions of working for the Park Service is actually working in the national parks. It is also a great opportunity to use your architectural and engineering skills. These skills are put to good use and further developed in the Park Service.

11

Resource Management

You've heard of business management, financial management, and personnel management, but what is resource management? Resource management is the maintenance, restoration, protection, and perpetuation of a park's resources.

In the national parks, we're concerned with both natural and cultural resources. Natural resources include native plants and animals, water, soils, and geologic features; cultural resources relate to our nation's history and culture. Cultural resources feature historic sites and buildings, archeological objects and ruins, outdoor statues and monuments, documents, and museum objects. For example, the resources of Yellowstone National Park are mostly natural—buffalo, elk, moose, trout, rivers, birds, and geology—while those of Gettysburg National Military Park are predominantly cultural, with its historic significance, monuments, and military artifacts.

For years, resource management was the primary job of the park ranger, who was obliged to budget his or her time to perform the dual tasks of visitor protection and resource management. Increased visitation required the ranger to spend more time on visitor protection. This led to the emergence in the early 1980s of a new specialist, the resource manager.

To give you an idea of what resource managers do,

let's look at some of their projects in the parks, then spend a day with a resource manager.

Dave Haskell is the resource manager at Shenandoah National Park in Virginia's Blue Ridge Mountains. The park is extremely popular for a variety of outdoor activities, including fishing, camping, and hiking. It features forty-two mountain streams, all containing wild brook trout. Every year, starting in June, Dave and his staff electroshock the streams to check the trout population. Streams with low populations are closed to fishing until the populations rebuild. Last year, twenty-eight of the streams were open to fishing. Dave's job as resource manager is to protect the resource, in this case brook trout, and to ensure its future.

Another resource management example occurred at George Washington's Birthplace National Monument near Fredericksburg, Virginia. Dwight Storke, now superintendent of the park, was resource manager a few years ago. Dwight studied everything he could find about the park and the colonial period in Virginia.

In his research, he found references to a species of flax that was grown on the grounds during Washington's time there. When he found this flax being grown in Minnesota, he had some seeds sent to him to plant in the park. Dwight wanted that garden and all other resources in the park to be historically accurate.

The resource manager's responsibility for a park's resources brings him into contact with the other divisions of the staff. Most resource management projects are actually carried out by people in other divisions, especially in small parks.

For example, the maintenance division works closely with the resource manager to control and eradicate exotic plants, like kudzu, which covers everything in its path. The interpretive division develops programs for the public to explain the importance of park resources

Resource Management

and how the presence of certain species are indicators of an ecosystem's health.

When Shenandoah wants to close some streams to fishing, the interpretive division develops a program to describe the importance of native brook trout to the park and what is being done to preserve the populations. The rangers and the resource manager collaborate to stop poaching in the park and to protect the public from wildlife and wildlife from the public during certain times of the year.

One of the attractions of a resource management career is the satisfaction of doing hands-on work with park resources and watching them flourish under your guidance.

For a broader view of a resource manager's responsibilities, let's spend a day with Steve Chaney at Mammoth Cave National Park in Kentucky. Steve supervises a staff of nine—one permanent employee, five seasonal employees, and three volunteers. He is responsible for visitor and resource protection in a park with 50,000 acres of backcountry, 70 miles of trails, 25 miles of river, over 200 separate caves, and over 350 miles of caves.

Steve's day starts at 7:30 A.M. On his way to the office, he stops at maintenance headquarters to meet with a trail maintenance crew and go over the final details for the removal of two hazardous trees. Steve had identified the trees along a park trail. One had been damaged by lightning, and the other was rotted at the base; both could fall at any time, possibly injuring or killing someone. Last week, Steve and the maintenance chief had agreed on a date to remove the trees, and yesterday Steve marked the trees with red marking tape. Part of one tree trunk will be left to create a habitat for cavity-nesting birds.

At 8:00, cup of coffee in hand, Steve attends the

superintendent's weekly staff meeting. During this meeting the management staff reports to the superintendent concerning their areas of responsibility. Steve reports that he has developed a cave use permit system to allow spelunkers to explore caves closed to the general public. The park staff monitors these sections. This ensures that visitors do not damage this resource. They can respond promptly with search and rescue operations if the explorers fail to return on schedule.

At 9:10 A.M., he drives two seasonal park technicians over to the Green River. The technicians are trained to take water-quality samples and temperature readings. Steve goes over the instructions one more time and sets them on a weekly schedule to record these data. He is trying to obtain funding to hire a seasonal hydrologic technician who can carry out the park's water-quality monitoring program.

At 10:30 A.M., Steve comes back to his office, where he returns phone calls and tries to whittle down the pile of paperwork on his desk. The bane of supervisors is paperwork: filling out forms, completing employee performance evaluations, recording program accomplishments, reviewing project proposals from other agencies, and answering information requests. Steve remembers his school days and pays special attention to information requests from children and college students. He makes every effort to give them what they need or to point them in the right direction.

At noon, he drives into town to have lunch with two friends and fellow biologists from the U.S. Fish and Wildlife Service and the Kentucky Department of Fish and Wildlife Resources. The three are working on a plan to restore nesting bald eagles to the Mammoth Cave area of Kentucky. They discuss the habitat requirements of the bald eagle, what sections of the park would best meet those needs, and the logistical prob-

Resource Management

lems of constructing and maintaining an eagle hacking site in the backcountry.

At 1:30 P.M., Steve picks up the chief of maintenance. They drive to the park's visitor center where the nonnative kudzu plant does what it does best—engulfing the trees and plants in its path. Kudzu covers vegetation like a blanket, eventually killing its host by blocking out light. Earlier in the year, Steve had arranged for five maintenance crew members to learn how to apply pesticides properly. Steve and the maintenance chief discuss the time and manpower involved in stopping the spread of kudzu. They schedule two pesticide applications for the following week. They then return to Steve's office to examine park topographic maps. Steve points out areas where he wants to restore native plants to control bank erosion along the Nolin River.

They are interrupted by an urgent call from the regional office in Atlanta seeking endangered species information. Within thirty minutes, Steve compiles the information from his files and calls the Atlanta office back. As soon as he hangs up, he receives a call from the Mather Training Center in Harpers Ferry, West Virginia, asking him to teach part of a training course on Remote Areas Management. He will be discussing cave management and visitor safety. They agree on times and dates, contingent upon the superintendent's approval.

By now it is 4:00 P.M., and Steve must schedule tomorrow's work for his seasonal rangers. He usually makes weekly schedules, but tomorrow he needs a special job done. The two seasonals must place nets in portions of First Creek Lake and collect fish population data. Two weeks earlier, Steve and the two seasonal rangers had placed nets in part of the lake and marked each fish caught in their nets by clipping a fin. Using a technique called mark and recapture, every fish caught in the net on the first trip is marked by clipping a fin. On the second trip, the same section of the lake is laid with nets. The number of marked fish caught the second time makes up a percentage of the total catch. Using this method, they can estimate the total number of fish in the lake.

At 4:30 P.M., he heads home, has an early dinner with his family, and watches his oldest son play in a Little League baseball game. When the game is over, Steve joins the park's superintendent at the County Supervisors meeting. They are working together to block a rezoning plan that would allow a large shopping center to be built next to the park.

Protecting park boundaries is a never-ending job for many park superintendents and resource managers. In years past, parks were virtual "islands," separate from bordering lands. Today, some of the most serious threats to park resources come from activities outside the park. To help remedy this, some conservationists have proposed that each park set up a buffer zone where construction is prohibited.

At the zoning meeting, Steve explains to the board members how major construction projects near the park would have negative effects on the park's resources. Site clearing for the shopping center would result in heavy sediment runoff from the Green River and its feeder creeks. This would suffocate the egg-laden nests of the bass, catfish, crappie, and bluegill and harm several endangered species of mussels. Animals would be displaced and native vegetation destroyed, allowing nonnative plants to invade the park. The air quality of the park would suffer further if the shopping center attracted the predicted crowds. But the most important point is that the construction could damage the underground cave labyrinth that makes Mammoth Cave world-famous.

Finally at 10:30, Steve arrives home for the short remainder of the evening, knowing that tomorrow will bring new situations and challenges. A resource manager's job is never boring, never routine, and never finished.

12

Scientists

How would you like to spend ten years studying the mechanisms of orogeny in the crystalline core of the North Cascades? This research deals with the process of mountain formation. That doesn't appeal to you? Another possibility is to spend a year monitoring the timber rattlesnake population of Shenandoah National Park. Those are just two of the thousands of research projects that Park Service scientists carry out or oversee.

Research is defined as a scholarly or systematic inquiry aimed at the discovery and interpretation of facts. Researchers revise accepted theories in light of new facts and develop practical applications of the new or revised theories. The national parks are wonderful laboratories for scientists. They compile valuable research which enables the superintendents to protect the park resources. Studies of mammals, geology, plants, reptiles, trees, and human behavior provide park managers with the scientific basis to make enlightened decisions.

Decisions on controversial issues such as the reintroduction of the gray wolf to Yellowstone National Park or the elimination of commercial fishing in Everglades National Park depend on research findings and analysis. Such decisions cannot be based on emotion but must be grounded in scientific fact.

Scientists direct and accomplish this research. Every NPS regional office has a regional chief scientist who oversees the ongoing and planned research for the parks. Large parks usually have one or two scientists dedicated to research. A few parks have enough scientists on staff to create a research division or center. These include the Uplands Research Center in Great Smoky Mountains National Park, the South Florida Research Center in Everglades National Park, and the research divisions in Yellowstone and Glacier National Parks. Most parks, however, either depend on scientists from nearby parks or contract with a university or an independent research scientist.

Park Service scientists also are based on college campuses in Cooperative Park Studies Units (CPSU). The Service establishes CPSUs in cooperation with universities to assist in conducting research to meet resource management needs. In most cases, the NPS scientist heads the CPSU. Otherwise the Service has an agreement with the university by which a faculty member serves part–time as CPSU head. The units report to the chief scientist in the regional office responsible for the parks served by that unit. Currently there are twenty-two CPSUs across the country.

Research scientist positions are usually in those parks where serious research problems exist or are perceived. Dr. Richard Weisbrod is the research scientist at St. Croix National Scenic Riverway, which lies on the northern border between Minnesota and Wisconsin. Currently, he supervises or coordinates seventeen research projects for the Park Service while actively conducting research on *Lyme borreliosis* and on neotropical migrating birds. The Saint Croix River Valley is a focal point for Lyme disease in the Upper Midwest, and Dr. Weisbrod's research is one of the few studies in the country examining the prevalence of the disease in mammalian populations. His studies on migrating birds in the Saint Croix Valley is contributing to a new understanding of neotropical migrant ecology.

According to Dr. Weisbrod, "Ideally the park management staff identifies and prioritizes the park's research needs. Our research schedule is based on a consensus reached by the park staff, the regional chief scientist, and myself." The Park Service has a small research budget, forcing scientists to seek outside funding. In fact, far more research is performed by researchers with outside funding than with Park Service funds.

"I write a lot of detailed project proposals trying to solicit funds from various sources outside the Park Service," says Dr. Weisbrod. Funding is available from such sources as the National Institute of Health and the National Science Foundation. "Other federal agencies, the states, private foundations, and universities fund research for the Park Service. You have to be aware of the alternative funding sources and your park's research needs and try to match the two."

Often lower-priority park or NPS projects are funded before higher research priorities. This is because the outside funding emphasis is on the lower-priority projects. As Dr. Weisbrod remarks, "Research emphasis is often placed where the money is available at the time." For independently funded research, the Park Service scientist reviews the proposal and makes a recommendation to the superintendent, who has final approval.

If the staff identifies a vital research need that is outside the scientist's expertise, the park contracts with the appropriate experts. Each research study, no matter who conducts it, must meet the following standards:

- Each research study must have a proposal that includes the purpose, objectives, and scientific

methodology of the study; precise identification of the study area, proposed starting and ending dates, and provisions for reporting the results.
- Studies must be scientifically valid and tested through peer review.
- Studies should contribute to a better understanding of park resources and ecosystems and their use and management.
- Specimen collection and destructive sampling are allowed only if they result in scientific knowledge not otherwise available or provide information for increased resource protection.
- Specimen collection must be accomplished by qualified representatives of agencies or institutions.

Park Service scientists also are subject to the pressures of the academic maxim, "Publish or perish." A research scientist's work is evaluated by an independent review board of peers known as a Research Grade Evaluation (RGE). It is a special classification system used to determine the grade and pay of federal employees engaged in natural science research.

Under the RGE system, a young PhD scientist enters federal employment as a GS-11 or GS-12. Through successful research and publications, he or she can advance to GS-18. This is the same way that academic researchers advance in a university tenure system. The RGE system works to the advantage of both the scientist and the federal government. The scientist is not locked into a grade or forced to transfer to another job to get a promotion, and the government is able to recruit and retain competent scientists.

A closely allied classification system is the Grants Grade Evaluation (GGE), which is used to determine the grade and pay scale of scientists engaged primarily in research administration. Because they administer research programs rather than conduct original research, regional chief scientists and some CPSU unit leaders are on the GGE system.

Some parks without research scientists on staff have professional resource managers who are capable of designing and managing a research program. These people hold an advanced degree in an appropriate scientific field. They are graded in the GS professional series. Parks without a resource manager have to depend on the regional chief scientist for help in developing research projects.

All of the research in the national parks is compiled each year in an inventory of research activities. Each researcher must complete an Investigators Annual Report and return it to the regional chief scientist, who then forwards it to headquarters in Washington.

13

Rescue Rangers

Butch Farabee was sure he was going to die. He was in Yosemite National Park trying to rescue two children trapped in a tree in the middle of the rainswollen Merced River. Their boat had wrapped around the tree, and the cold spray from the water slapping against the boat and the tree was dousing the ten-year-old boy and his eight-year-old sister. Hypothermia was approaching.

A former state champion swimmer, Farabee knew that he had to act quickly before the kids lost their grip. He tied a rope to a tree and started swimming toward them. The raging current swept him off course and toward a fallen tree sticking out of the water. If the river swept him under the tree, he could be trapped and drowned. As the current sucked him under the trunk, he grabbed hold of it as he went under. "This is it," thought Butch, "I'm going to die." He had one chance. Using every bit of strength in his muscular upper body, he launched himself against the tide and onto the top of the trunk. As Butch describes it, "I hulked myself out." Catching his breath and resting momentarily, he went back to his original plan and successfully rescued the children.

In his twenty-five-year career with the Park Service, Butch Farabee has been involved in over 1,000 rescues. "There have been dozens of times when I thought I was going to die," says Farabee, "but I loved helping to save lives, and the risk is part of the job." Butch currently works as the superintendent of Padre Island National Seashore in Texas and leads a more sedate life. Previously he rangered in Yosemite and Grand Canyon National Parks, two hotbeds of search-and-rescue (SAR) activity.

The large mountainous parks in the West such as Grand Teton, Mount Rainier, Lassen, Grand Canyon, Yosemite, and Yellowstone have busy search-and-rescue programs. These parks attract mountain and rock climbers in droves. Unfortunately, not all of them are skilled, and many need rescuing. Even experienced climbers have an occasional accident and need help, but you can count on the novice climbers to get in trouble.

Yosemite averages 125 to 150 rescue missions each year. Rangers with an affinity for mountain climbing are drawn to these parks and sharpen their skills for use in SAR operations. Water-based parks like Lake Mead Amistad Recreation Area, Indiana Dunes, and Glen Canyon require different skills of their SAR teams: strong swimmers, scuba divers, and experienced boaters.

Saving lives takes precedence over all other Park management priorities. Congress specifically directed the Park Service to provide for public use of the parks, and the Service assumes responsibility for the welfare of the persons using these areas.

National Park Service SAR has evolved into a sophisticated program. Search–and–rescue operations are carefully planned to optimize the use of staff and equipment. The Park Service uses a methodology known as the Incident Command System (ICS). Originally developed in southern California for wildland firefighting, ICS is a standardized system to determine who is the lead agency or person in situations such as fire, searches, or law enforcement. Many federal agencies use the system to break down a problem into component parts and manage each part with the appropriate staff and resources. With ICS, there is one commander and everyone knows his or her own role.

The chief ranger of each park is responsible for SAR operations. In large parks, the chief ranger may designate another ranger as SAR coordinator. Individual park staffs identify their typical problems and situations and develop training and techniques to respond to them. Part of the ICS process is working out agreements (Memorandums of Understanding, or MOUs) with other federal and local agencies to provide support during SAR operations. For example, a nearby National Forest may have a helicopter. The park and the National Forest sign an MOU by which the Forest Service provides the helicopter in exchange for reimbursable expenses or help from the park SAR rangers in rescuing visitors on national forest lands. MOUs with local agencies provide manpower or equipment from the local sheriff's department, state police, or national guard.

This planning with other agencies and individuals pays off during a search–and–rescue mission. Recently two young marines from the Twenty-Nine Palms Marine Base in California were with some friends exploring the area around Joshua Tree National Monument. Cruising on three-wheel vehicles, the marines became separated from their friends and strayed into the park. Stranded when the vehicles ran out of gas, the marines decided to walk to safety. Dressed in tank tops and without drinking water, they faced desert temperatures of 105 degrees and ground temperatures above 130 degrees.

Early the next day, their friends reported them overdue. The park initiated a major search, calling on help from both local trackers and the Marine Base. Ground searchers, helicopters, and dog teams combed the desert until late that night, when a ranger tracking team found the two men. The rescue team began treating them for dehydration and hypothermia until a marine helicopter arrived and evacuated them to the base hospital. The successful rescue was a coordinated effort among many groups planned in advance and directed by the Park Service Incident Commander.

Search–and–rescue responsibilities may be required as part of a ranger's job description, but SAR is not a full–time job. Most of the rangers involved in SAR are there because of their interest in it. In Yosemite, Butch describes SAR duty as "a process of self-selection." Rangers interested in mountain climbing wanted to be part of the team. When Butch led SAR in Yosemite, interested rangers were brought along slowly until they were fully prepared. They often got together after work to practice climbing and simulate rescues.

Most of the SAR training is park-specific. Yosemite rangers train for mountain and river rescue, whereas Lake Mead rangers practice for open-water and boat-oriented rescue. Each year the Park Service sponsors national training courses for SAR. Recently it sponsored a river-rescue training course at New River Gorge National River in West Virginia.

The Park Service also sponsors courses in Emergency Medical Services (EMS). Often people who are rescued need immediate medical attention. Some rangers are trained in procedures such as setting up an IV to give fluids to people suffering from dehydration.

State and local groups also give courses that Park Service employees attend such as air reconnaissance, tracking with dog teams, and human tracking. The Service also takes advantage of opportunities with the military in medevac training and helicopter-rappelling. Many rangers, sparked by their own interest, attend courses provided by other agencies. Butch Farabee, for example, has over 400 hours of SCUBA training. The

RESCUE RANGERS

Mountain rescue at Yosemite National Park (National Park Service).

most valuable form of training is OJT—on-the-job training. Nothing is better than experience in search–and–rescue.

Even an experienced ranger occasionally needs rescuing. Now superintendent of Canyonlands National Park in Utah, Walt Dabney started his career in Yosemite under Butch Farabee's tutelage. Walt scaled a spectacular cliff without ropes to seach for a visitor who had fallen into a creek. He was struck with vertigo while climbing on a high rock face. He had a difficult time maintaining his balance, and was unable to move up or down. While waiting to be rescued, Walt moved sideways but fell. He stopped himself by holding onto a narrow crack with two fingers and then worked himself back to his original positon. Another climber was finally able to get a rope down to him, and he climbed out. This near-fatal encounter did not deter Walt at all. He went on to lead SAR operations in Mount Rainier, Grand Teton, and Everglades.

SAR operations are expensive in terms of both manpower hours and equipment. The use of helicopters is particularly costly. But costs take a back seat to saving lives. The Park Service usually does not charge victims for costs incurred during SAR operations; it absorbs the expenses with help from the Washington and regional offices. Individuals, organizations, and other agencies donate time and effort. In 1994, $1,381,000 was donated toward SAR efforts by volunteers and the military.

Grand Canyon National Park charges visitors up to $500 for SAR operations. Grand Canyon, however, is a unique situation. The majority of rescues require a helicopter, and the charges are for helicopter use. The combination of rugged terrain, high temperatures, and inexperienced visitors keeps the SAR teams and the helicopters busy throughout the year.

Most incidents occur because of inexperience. Visitors head into the canyon without the right equipment (usually the wrong shoes) and not enough water. They get off the trails, ignore common sense, and exceed their capabilities. This can result in hypothermia or heat exhaustion or prostration, all of which require immediate medical care. Grand Canyon has the highest number of medical assist emergencies in the entire park system.

Trying to save a life at Grand Canyon, Butch Farabee almost lost his own. Toward dusk, a young woman accidentally stepped backward over a 400-foot cliff. When the call came to the dispatch office, Butch responded immediately by driving to the overlook area. It was too late to put the helicopter up. Butch had his climbing gear in the trunk, so he rigged a 150-foot rope and lowered himself to see if the victim was still alive. More rescuers arrived and did not see Butch's rope in the dark. Preparing to descend, they created an avalanche of rocks toward Butch dangling below. Avoiding the rocks was hard enough, but the avalanche was causing his rope to fray. Spotting a ledge, he swung over and gained a foothold. The other rescuers were surprised to hear his voice shouting to them for another rope. They complied, and Butch quickly climbed out. He was lucky. Unfortunately, the young woman was not: her body was recovered by the helicopter the next morning.

Despite every effort by the interpretive rangers to educate visitors about the dangers in the parks and the all-out efforts of the SAR rangers, fatalities are a fact of life. But the rangers still win more than they lose. In 1994, SAR rangers responded to 4,593 incidents involving 5,813 persons. Although there were 170 fatalities, the SAR rangers were directly responsible for saving 773 lives.

No matter how trained or experienced the rangers are, each rescue is different and has its own hidden dangers. SAR work is analogous to driving a race car. Although drivers expect to finish every race, there is no guarantee that they will not be injured or killed at any time. SAR offers the same roll of the dice.

Rangers stoically accept the danger inherent in SAR activities. Butch Farabee says, "It's a cliché to say that danger is part of being a ranger. But it is. We knew about the danger when we signed on for search-and-rescue, so we made the choice. The reward is saving a life. Nothing compares to saving a life." Often the people rescued stay in touch with their rescuers, sending high school graduation photos, wedding pictures, and Christmas cards. Butch Farabee gets a lot of Christmas cards.

14

Historians

Drifting slowly along the shoreline of the Yazoo River, Ed Bearss knew he was close. His painstaking research of the Vicksburg battle records and hours of studying river maps were about to pay off. He watched the compass needle intently for any indication of metal, ready with the long thin rod to probe the mud below. When the needle jumped, Ed thrust the rod through the mud and struck iron. This iron, however, was more important to him than gold. After a year's research, Ed had found the ironclad Civil War ship named *Cairo*, which had been sunk during operations before the Battle of Chickasaw Bayou. The discovery of the Union Army gunboat is considered one of the most important discoveries associated with the Civil War.

At the time, Ed was the park historian at Vicksburg National Military Park in Mississippi. Later he became the nationally known chief historian of the National Park Service. He has authored more than a dozen books, and has been featured prominently in Ken Burns's Civil War television documentary.

Ed went on to direct the salvage of the *Cairo* and on his own time carefully recorded and safeguarded its priceless collection of historic artifacts. His initiative and research has been a great contribution to our knowledge of the events.

There may be more *Cairos* out there in one form or another. For historians, the national parks are a gold mine, with nuggets scattered throughout ready to be unearthed. There is so much to study, learn, and share with the public not only in the historical parks but also in the scenic parks. Historical parks are many and varied, from battlefields to Presidential birthplaces and homes, to Native American sites and parks commemorating the growth of our country. "Education is our goal," says Ed. "The historian's primary role is to interpret the park's resources and mission to the public."

Two types of historians are in the Park Service: research historians and interpretive ranger historians. Research historians gear their work to the needs of a park. One may track an army battalion's movements during a battle; another may write a biography of a building.

Ed Trout, park historian at Great Smoky Mountains National Park in Tennessee and North Carolina, has written separate biographies of many of the eighty historic buildings in the park. Known as Historic Structure Reports, they tell the life story of a building. By seeking old photographs and conducting interviews with the people who built or lived in the structure or their descendants, the unique story of each building is unveiled. From these stories spring interpretive programs, living history demonstrations, and correct preservation and maintenance methods. In the Cades Cove section of the Great Smokies, Ed's research led the interpreters to develop a living history program that included a grist mill and a country store, and demonstrations of blacksmithing, weaving, and spinning.

Dan Brown at Cumberland Gap National Historical Park, in Virginia, Kentucky, and Tennessee, is also researching old buildings. A highway tunnel is being constructed in the park, and Dan is researching the buildings in the tunnel area to see if they qualify for nomination to the National Register of Historic Places.

All historians are familiar with the National Historic Preservation Act of 1966. Section 106 of the Act requires federal agencies to consider the effects of their actions on historic properties. The purpose is to avoid unnecessary damage from federal actions.

National Historic Landmarks are buildings, structures, sites, objects, or districts designated by the Secretary of the Interior because of their importance in American history, architecture, archeology, engineering, or culture. The National Register of Historic Places is similar except that the sites usually are of state, regional, or local importance. The National Park Service administers the Landmarks and National Register programs.

If Dan discovers that any of the buildings meet the criteria for designation as a historic place, the Park Service will examine ways to protect them from any damage resulting from the tunnel construction.

In his research, Dan established a library in the park to house the data accumulated in building a historical record of the park resources. "I truly believe that each park needs a library to build a resource base," he emphasizes. "Among the materials in our library are the complete land acquisition files for the park, which we recovered and preserved." As a result, the Park Service has not lost a land dispute at Cumberland Gap.

Research is also prompted by visitor requests for historical information. At Fredericksburg and Spotsylvania County Military Parks in Virginia, historian Don Pfanz responds to numerous requests. The park is composed of parts of four battlefields (Fredericksburg, Chancellorsville, Wilderness, Spotsylvania Court House), and visitors typically want to know where an ancestor fought and possibly died.

"Give me his name and state," says Don, "and if he fought for the Confederates we can usually find his regiment." Tracking a person in the Union Army is a bit harder because the North had so many more regiments. "For the Union Army, we need the name of the soldier and his regiment."

Over the years, park historians have assembled their regimental histories from battle reports filed by the officers of each army. Information gaps are filled through personal memoirs and letters from soldiers giving the locations and actions of their regiments. One of the best sources of these memoirs and letters are the visitors themselves. The park actively seeks and collects unpublished manuscripts about the battles and the Civil War in general. If a visitor remarks that a relative fought in one of the four battles, the park staff ask whether the relative left any accounts of the battle. Enough people have sent in copies of manuscripts that the collection currently numbers between 15,000 and 20,000 documents.

What does a park historian do besides research? "Research! I wish I had time to do more research," Pfanz laughs. "Day-to-day duties and projects take most of my time. Research is so time-consuming that few parks have the luxury to do a lot of it." Don is in charge of all the nonpersonal interpretation in the park. He writes the text for the interpretive signs, and has written the script for two of the taped tours of the battlefields. A new project entails writing pamphlets on other battlefields in the regions that are not managed by the Park Service. The park is producing the pamphlets to bring attention to less well-known battlegrounds such as Brandy Station or Yellow Tavern in the hope that increased visibility will help to preserve them from the developer's shovel and bulldozer.

Every few months, Don takes a day walking and

driving around the park to "see the park through the visitors' eyes" and ensure that the signs, buildings, and historic scenes are up to standard. Listing every deficiency from a broken sign to a building in need of paint, he works with the appropriate park division (usually maintenance) to correct the problem.

Although he no longer does interpretive programs regularly, Don still gives tours to special groups, often military officers from the nearby Quantico Marine Base or from the Pentagon, which is only 90 minutes away. Known as "staff rides," these battlefield tours for military brass were popular until 1940, when they stopped. Ed Bearss helped restore their popularity in 1985 by leading the Secretary of the Army and a score of his senior generals on a tour of Antietam Battlefield. Employees of the Department of the Interior and the Park Service in Washington are treated twice a year to a tour of nearby Civil War–related sites.

Most research historians help the interpretive rangers with the accuracy of information. They also provide interpretive training. Dan Brown is an instructor for black-powder weapons. Terry Winschel, research historian at Vicksburg, trains interpreters to care for and maintain audiovisual equipment and to develop living history programs. Depending on their specialty, historians are expected to help with in-house training.

Historians also write administrative histories of the parks, documenting the legislation establishing the park, the politics and controversies that influenced the legislation, fund-raising efforts by the proponents and opponents of the park, and how the park developed.

Public speaking, editing manuscripts, answering information requests, and writing take up any other time a historian may have. Terry Winschel is a frequent speaker on the Vicksburg lunch circuit, describing aspects of the Vicksburg siege to local Civil War groups and service organizations. Terry maintains the park's archival collection of over 12,000 documents and more than 5,000 photographs. He also edits manuscripts for publications such as *National Geographic*, and reviews books for newspapers and magazines. Employees at Vicksburg are encouraged to write, and Terry, in addition to his own writing, assists them in preparing articles and interpretive brochures for publication. Historians also write portions of each park's interpretive plan and cultural resource management plan.

In contrast to research historians, the interpretive ranger historians interact with the public every day through their programs. Battlefield tours are a regular part of the ranger's job. Thoroughly knowing the history of a park and reading the available literature are expected of all ranger historians, but Ed Bearss believes that to understand and know a historical area, especially a battlefield, you must walk the ground. "Although historians may be familiar with the literature, they cannot truly appreciate the challenges faced by our forebears until they walk the ground."

Bearss practices what he preaches. In 1969, after being assigned the study on the proposed Klondike Gold Rush National Historical Park, Ed spent three days alone hiking the Chilkoot Trail, sleeping under the stars and sustaining himself on cans of sardines, which a friend had told him were light to carry. His hike is known in the Park Service as the "Great Sardine March."

On another occasion, Ed was assigned to study submerged shipwrecks near Fort Jefferson in the Dry Tortugas. On his own time, Bearss took scuba diving lessons, allowing him to visit the underwater sites he was researching.

Historians

The challenge for any interpreter is to make programs lively, educational, and entertaining. In an effort to convey to the visitor the importance of the event, ranger historians often make period clothing and equipment for their living history demonstrations. "The park is your classroom," says Ed. "You must make history come alive because if no enthusiasm is generated in the group, the historian's knowledge of the park and the literature will not be shared." And that is what Park Service historians do best—share their knowledge.

15

Archeologists

"I feel very fortunate to work for the Park Service," says Mark Lynott, as he explains the diverse archeological projects in the parks. Mark is the Midwest regional archeologist, based at the Midwest Archeological Center in Lincoln, Nebraska. "The Park Service provides an outstanding career opportunity for archeologists because it is oriented to resource preservation rather than development, and there are so many potential sites in the parks yet to be discovered."

Archeology is an interpretive science dedicated to the study of man's past by examining the physical remains of his activities. Using careful excavation techniques to discover artifacts, archeologists are able to construct scenarios of daily life many generations ago.

Due to land modification in the form of urban growth, highways, reservoirs, and agriculture, a large number of archeological sites have been destroyed and many more are currently threatened. Much archeological work being done today is "salvage" work, with scientists racing against time to preserve and record the earth's artifacts and stories before the sites are destroyed. As sites disappear, the national parks assume added importance. Through a combination of federal laws and Park Service policies, the parks are today considered to be archeological preserves.

Park Service archeologists are rarely stationed in the

parks. Most work out of regional offices or a facility like the Midwest Archeological Center or the Southwest Cultural Resources Center in Santa Fe, New Mexico.

The Midwest Center, for instance, is a research office that provides archeological services, regulatory compliance with state and federal laws, and management advice to the thirty-two parks in the ten-state region. The majority of its work involves helping planners identify and evaluate the archeological resources in park areas proposed for development. In the park development zones, identified in the GMP and other planning documents, the planners may consider alternate locations for construction of any number of structures such as employee housing, visitor centers, concessions facility, or park administration buildings.

The center archeologists do surveying and often site-testing in the development area. In a survey phase, the archeologists try to find sites that might be affected by construction. If such a site is found, it is evaluated to see if it is eligible for the National Register of Historic Places. If the site is considered significant in any way, the archeologists, planners, and park managers work together to try to minimize the construction impact or possibly relocate the development. If the site cannot be avoided, the archeologists do a data recovery excavation to rescue information before development. Although much of the work is related to proposed construction, survey and testing are also initiated to gather information for long-term management and for public interpretation. The goals of site survey and site testing involving excavation are similar: to collect data that can help reconstruct the history and living conditions of the early human habitations.

Besides work on prehistoric sites, much of the archeological work involves research on historic sites dating from the early eighteenth to the late nineteenth

San Francisco high school students help Park Service archeologists excavate a Civil War gun emplacement at Fort Mason in the Golden Gate National Recreation Area (Richard Frear photo, National Park Service).

centuries. In the process of restoring historic structures, archeologists recover materials that provide clues to the activities or events that occurred at the site. In attempting to recreate a scenario of life at the site, archeologists examine the location of artifacts as closely as the artifact itself. "Collecting artifacts is not an end in itself," comments Vergil Noble, an archeologist at the Midwest Center. "We can learn a lot from the location of an artifact in relation to the historic structure and other artifacts. The information yielded is often more important than the artifact."

Steering a different course from excavation for data recovery, Mark recently completed a site stabilization project at Voyageurs National Park in Minnesota. Widespread shoreline erosion was eating away at some of the more significant archeological sites in the park. Rather than undertake the costs of large-scale data recovery and curation of the artifacts, Mark directed a winter stabilization effort. Using a filter fabric and turf-stabilization matting in conjunction with large amounts of sediment and riprap, Mark produced a new shoreline that will protect the identified archeological deposits.

Archeology does not always involve digging to recover artifacts. The Submerged Cultural Resources Unit of the Southwest Cultural Resources Center conducts research on underwater resources throughout the park system, with emphasis on historic shipwrecks. Led by Dan Lenihan, unit members use their underwater archeology skills to explore, measure, photograph, decipher, and sketch these important components of a park's resource base.

"We're a technical team working to evaluate historic properties," explains Dan. "We are the only underwater archeological team in the Park Service, so we work all over the United States." Their work has taken them from the warm waters of the Dry Tortugas to explore the shipwrecks near Fort Jefferson to the frigid waters of the Great Lakes to catalog shipwrecks off of Apostle Islands National Lakeshore and Isle Royale National Park. They also worked with the U.S. Navy to gather information on the battleships USS *Arizona* and USS *Utah*, sunk at Pearl Harbor.

Like the land sites, there is no shortage of underwater sites. As Dan reveals, "Consider that even without a formal inventory of sites, we can recognize underwater archeological needs in at least sixty areas of the national park system, including marine, Great Lakes, riverine, karst, and reservoir environments. The total number of sites is well into the thousands."

Back on the surface, archeological work is going on at parks throughout the country. Archeologists at the

Archeologists

NPS divers work on a shipwreck in Guam (National Park Service).

Grand Canyon spend considerable time working with the resources of the inner canyon. Projects include stabilizing prehistoric and historic ruins, doing inventory surveys, excavating endangered sites, and monitoring sites along the river and backcountry trails. Work in the Grand Canyon requires extensive planning. Sites are rarely located within easy access. Logistical support may be in the form of pack mules, a raft along the Colorado River, or the park helicopter. New sites are discovered regularly. A survey of 5 percent of the park yielded 2,300 sites.

Because archeology is an interpretive science, park resources provide a basis for a variety of interpretive programs. To this end, park archeologists help the interpreters develop programs for archeology.

Much of their time is taken up with the paperwork required by legal and regulatory compliance and with scientific reports detailing the findings at the sites. "New archeologists go through a tough period learning the regulatory compliance requirements," Mark comments. "They want to dig holes and find bones, not deal with paperwork and compliance issues. College doesn't train archeologists in the practicalities of cultural resource management, so they learn it on the job."

They also learn that employees of the Park Service have a real commitment to their jobs and the goal of preserving the parks' resources.

16

Dispatchers

Park visitors never get to see some of the most important Park Service employees. Hidden in locked rooms at their respective parks, dispatchers play a vital role in the daily operations of the national parks.

Amid their telephones, computers, multichannel radios, paging encoders, and various other technical equipment, the dispatchers orchestrate the daily happenings in the park. They direct radio traffic on networks which link everyone from rangers to maintenance workers to the county sheriff's department.

If a hiker in Grand Canyon National Park is injured, the dispatcher becomes part of the rescue team. If rangers are chasing car thieves in the park, the dispatcher becomes part of the chase. The job is rarely routine or boring, which is part of its attractiveness. "I like the aspect of coming to work and never knowing what my day will be like," says Deb Frauson, the dispatch supervisor at Grand Teton National Park. She had an idea of what she was getting into when she was hired on at the dispatch office. Previously Deb had worked as a 911 Operator for a county agency, where she acquired firsthand knowledge of the stress that often accompanies the job. The dispatcher job was her first full-time job with the Park Service after working for three years as a seasonal employee. She now supervises a staff of two year–round dispatchers and four seasonals.

"In Grand Teton, the dispatcher's chair is a hot seat," explains Deb. "The information is flying at you fast and furious, and you have to digest it, remain cool, and make the right decisions."

Everything that happens in a city happens in a park. Dispatchers handle all 911 emergency phone calls, quickly putting people and resources in action to respond. If you need medical assistance, a ranger is sent until a helicopter or ambulance arrives. If a fire starts, the local fire department or a park fire suppression team arrives. The dispatcher must be intimately familiar with the park, its geography, and its emergency resources as well as with park and local jurisdictions. If an emergency happens at Slough Creek Campground in Yellowstone National Park, the dispatcher has to know that Slough Creek is the North District and that the Sheriff's Department in nearby Cooke City, Montana, can provide assistance.

Dispatchers monitor all radio traffic in the park and from local agencies outside the park. Through radio monitoring, they keep tabs on all situations and keep the staff informed. Upon learning that a certain campground is full, the dispatcher relays that fact to the information desks at the visitor center or the entrance stations so visitors are apprised of available camping.

By monitoring the county sheriff's radio, they know of serious incidents outside the park and can radio the rangers for help. If the sheriff is pursuing a suspect toward the park, the dispatchers warn the rangers that trouble is coming their way. Generally, the parks and the local law-enforcement agencies work well together and constantly help each other.

In some parks, dispatchers also handle the telephone systems, switching thousands of calls daily. Imagine yourself sitting in the hot seat at Grand Canyon National Park with two switchboards, five radio channels

Dispatchers

in the park, and two channels for the sheriff's department and the concessioners.

Besides the radios and emergency phones, dispatchers must be computer-literate. The dispatch office has a computer connected to the National Crime Information Center (NCIC). Rangers call by radio for vehicle or license checks on cars they have stopped. The dispatcher quickly runs the check through NCIC. If the car is stolen or the person is wanted, the dispatcher uses a code that alerts the ranger to danger while the dispatcher sends backup units.

Do you need basic park information? The dispatch office has it. After park office hours at Yellowstone National Park, the dispatchers handle visitor information requests, providing basic facts such as opening and closing hours, campground availability, and where you can get gas or lodging.

A dispatcher's life is hectic during the summer, the busiest visitor season. It's not unusual for a dispatcher to have a phone in each ear, have a rescue in progress, and be responding to a radio call while listening to a potential problem on another radio. "We constantly prioritize multiple requests," explains Deb. It is similar to prioritizing in a hospital emergency room where doctors and nurses decide who needs immediate help and who can wait.

Properly prioritizing crisis situations comes with experience. According to Frauson, "It's at least a year before you feel somewhat comfortable as a dispatcher. Each situation is different, so each one is a learning experience. Situations spring up that you've never dealt with before. As a result, you learn from them."

Dispatchers play a crucial role during rescue operations. In a typical rescue situation, the dispatcher gets a call from a member of the party in trouble or a witness to the incident. Dispatchers are trained to extract specific information from the caller: who, what, where, and when. They put this information together and relay it to the lead ranger (Incident Commander) for that area. Upon direction from the Incident Commander, dispatchers start lining up the necessary resources. They put the helicopter on standby, stage the ambulance, notify backup rescuers to be ready, and alert the medical center about the type of injuries to expect. During the rescue, dispatchers keep communications flowing between the rescuers and the resources. Deb cautions, "You have to be clear and concise. You can't make assumptions or interpretations of what people are saying. You must know exactly what is said and what is needed, because someone's life depends on your clarity."

For significant incidents, the park staff examines and critiques the response and rescue, looking for ways to improve. The dispatch office is involved in this review. "We are our own worst critics," Deb says, "and the incident reviews are a good way for dispatchers to receive feedback from the rangers."

Similar to search and rescue operations, dispatchers help in park fires by serving as a link between the firefighters and supplies. The dispatcher deals with all communication needs of the firefighters and orders all the necessary materials for the next day or the next week. The magnitude of the Yellowstone fires in 1988 necessitated a separate dispatch office just for firefighter communications.

Not every situation is a crisis. More common are the mundane calls. This past September in Yellowstone, my fishing partner and I were fishing the picnic grounds section of the Lamar River when a thunderstorm moved in. We left the river reluctantly, because the trout were greedily attacking our dry flies. In a rush to stash our equipment and get out of the rain and lightning, my

Dispatchers

partner locked our keys in the trunk. The rain poured down raw and cold. The only natural cover was a copse of trees, which I don't recommend in a lightning storm. The other cover available was the concrete outhouse, which I don't recommend either, but it was safer than standing out in the open. Miracle of miracles, another fisherman pulled in and invited us into his car that was equipped with a car phone. We called dispatch, and within an hour a ranger arrived to open the locked car for two sheepish fishermen.

When prioritizing incidents, our keys-locked-in-car fiasco ranks at the bottom, but how about a situation where a river rescue, a mountain search–and–rescue, a law-enforcement incident, and a fire all happen on the same day? Rare though they are, such days can raise the stress level of the coolest dispatcher. Constantly working with intense situations causes burnout among dispatchers. All individuals have their own threshold.

Do dispatchers ever have easy days? When the visitor season is over, most park employees return to a normal life, including the dispatchers. Winters are less chaotic, with fewer search–and–rescue incidents. Winter is also a time to catch up on paperwork and attend training classes. As if they didn't have enough to do, the Grand Teton dispatchers help the rangers by processing all law-enforcement documents, including arrest citations and warnings. They also prepare files for court cases against persons arrested in the park. Just when life seems normal there comes a call to search for two overdue snowmobilers.

Life would be much easier for dispatchers if they only had to summon a wrecker service, deal with locked cars, or respond to the fisherman with a hook in his ear. But that would take the excitement out of the job and lessen the satisfaction of helping the visitors and playing a pivotal role in operating the park.

17

Fire Management

Firefighting in the National Park Service is a highly technical skill. Firefighting experience is fundamental to a career in most resource management positions, and it has become increasingly mandatory for managerial positions as one rises in the organization. Wildland fire management has evolved into a science-based program, with Park Service employees trained in fire behavior, suppression techniques, and the logistics of supplying the firefighters with food and equipment.

Work on the fireline is arduous, requiring long hours and a high level of physical fitness, discipline, and teamwork. Firefighting is a very hazardous occupation, although intensive training and proven fire suppression strategies greatly reduce the danger. Employees receive this training before they are allowed to engage in any fire-related activity. The Park Service does not intentionally expose firefighters to unsafe conditions without managing the risk.

Firefighting is done in concert with many other federal, state, and local agencies. Large wildfires, such as the Yellowstone fires of 1988, require a complex organization of trained professionals to combat the fire and limit the damage. At the height of the Yellowstone fires, 10,000 firefighters were at work. Various tactics are used to attack wildfires, but they generally aim at cutting off the spread of the fire, working from the origin around to the head of the fire, establishing a fireline (a cleared strip of land in front of a fire), and burning the area between the fireline and the fire.

Firefighters on the front lines spend a lot of time with shovels and pulaskis (a combination grub hoe and ax), building firelines. The high winds and intensity of the Yellowstone fires negated a lot of the hard work that went into building the firelines, carrying flames and sparks over them to spread the fire. Shifts of sixteen hours were not uncommon. Some nights, fire crews slept on the ground without dinner because supply helicopters couldn't land in the heavy smoke.

All firefighting is directed by the Incident Commander at a command base. The chain of command is determined by the Incident Command System (ICS), a complex structure that identifies all the positions required to manage and suppress the fire and support the effort. The qualifications for each job in the system are a combination of training and experience. An employee begins with the basics and over time builds qualifications toward higher-level positions.

The Incident Commander gives orders to the supervisors of the fire crews and plans their offensive and defensive actions. In addition to the actual firefighting personnel, medical and logistical staffs support the fire crews. Logistics people prepare the meals and provide other necessities such as lodging, equipment supply and repair, and mail delivery.

Firefighting is not a full-time job in the Park Service. Most positions have more than one area of responsibility, and the additional responsibilities are known as collateral duties. An employee's main position may be resource management, but the collateral duties might include firefighting, search–and–rescue, or interpretation. Employees spend most of their time on the

Fire Management

specific tasks of their position, but when a fire call comes, they respond.

How do you get started as a firefighter? You need a red card, which is obtained by completing basic firefighting courses and passing an aerobic fitness test. The training courses are Basic Fire Orientation, Firefighter Training, and Introduction to Fire Behavior.

How does a ranger at Shenandoah wind up fighting fires in Yellowstone? When a fire starts, the Incident Commander uses the nearest available forces. A park firefighting team may be able to suppress the fire, but if not, the closest available help is recruited. If more help is needed, a regional geographic center is called upon to provide logistical support in the way of firefighters and equipment. There are eleven of these centers throughout the United States, and they keep an up-to-date status board of available personnel and equipment in their region. The centers are coordinated by a National Interagency Coordination Center (NICC) at the Boise Interagency Fire Center in Idaho. When a region's resources begin to dry up, NICC directs supply efforts by moving people and material among the geographic centers. When more firefighters are needed, the ranger in Shenandoah may be directed by his geographic center to pack his gear and get to Yellowstone.

Firefighting responsibilities are traditional in the Park Service, but the use of prescribed fire has accelerated in recent years. Fire is used as a management tool in the parks, and some employees are trained to manage prescribed fire. A prescribed fire, formerly known as a controlled burn, is a fire set in a definite area under predetermined weather and fuel conditions to achieve a specific result.

Great advances have been made in predicting fire behavior. By measuring the current weather, the natural fuels (downed trees, leaves, pine needles, brush), and the terrain, computer programs are used to display fire specifics such as flame lengths, scorch heights, and how fast the fire will spread. Using this information, prescribed fire managers can predict how a fire will react before it is ignited.

The Park Service uses prescribed fires for a variety of management purposes. In historic areas, fire is used to keep vegetation in check and maintain a point in time for the historic scene. Trees and brush intrude onto the park area, and fire removes them, returning the area to its condition during the time of its historic significance.

Prescribed fire is also used to reduce hazards by burning a buffer zone, similar to a fireline, around important buildings or other structures in the park. Resource managers use prescribed fire to return an area to its natural fire frequency. Some prairies that have historically burned by natural wildfire about every twenty years haven't burned in sixty-five years. The resource manager tries to return the area to its natural fire frequency by burning it. It is hoped that natural fire will then take over and put the prairie back on the twenty-year frequency.

When the fire manager has determined the desired results of a prescribed fire, he develops a prescription. The prescription is a written statement which defines the objectives of the fire, the fuel and environmental conditions under which the fire will burn, and the specified final size of the fire.

When all the prescription conditions have been met, the fire is ignited and carefully monitored by trained and equipped firefighting crews. If the conditions change during the burn and move outside of the prescription, the fire is quickly suppressed.

All the attention so far has been on fighting wildland fires, but Park Service firefighters are also trained to

FIRE MANAGEMENT

Firefighters put in long days during the Yellowstone fires in 1988 (Jeff Henry photo, National Park Service).

fight structural fires. The Service is the third-largest owner of buildings in the nation, with over 16,000 structures. Fire protection for these structures is a major responsibility. Many of the parks have agreements with city or volunteer fire departments to provide protection, but in some cases no fire department is nearby. In these cases, selected park employees are trained in structural firefighting. The park sets up a fire brigade with a fire engine and the appropriate equipment.

As you can imagine, firefighting is not a profession that appeals to everyone. Training, experience, and physical fitness are the three key elements of a safe and successful career as a firefighter. Firefighting has become very scientific in the past two decades. Students interested in the career should be prepared to develop their mathematical, biological, and computer analysis skills. This background will help them to progress from the firefighter level to the Incident Commander Type I level (the highest single incident command position), which usually takes about fifteen years.

If you are interested in a career working with fire, contact the nearest National Park office for information and guidance to reference material. *Fire in America: A Cultural History of Wildland and Rural Fire* by Stephen Pyne is the premier work on the subject. He has also written *Fire on the Rim,* which describes a firefighter's responsibilities and dangers during one fire season at the Grand Canyon.

18

Public Affairs Officers

With fires raging in Yellowstone National Park, hundreds of reporters flocked to the scene, and the political heat carried all the way to Washington. Throughout it all, Joan Anzelmo stayed cool. Her position as the Public Affairs (PA) Officer at Yellowstone requires her to remain calm under pressure. But the summer fires of 1988 gave literal meaning to the expression "cool under fire," and aptly described her daily dealings with the media.

Usually a crisis is short-lived, but the Yellowstone fires went on for over three months, overwhelming the six-person PA office. Joan borrowed thirty-five people from Yellowstone's divisions and other parks to help handle the crush of reporters scrambling for stories. Over sixty-five fire information officers at the ten fire base camps throughout the park filed daily reports to her office, so she knew exactly what was happening in any given part of the vast park. To relay the information to the news media, she held daily press conferences. "One of the problems with so many reporters is that everyone wants a private interview with the superintendent," explains Joan. "We can't show favoritism to the networks or reporters, so we scheduled news conferences with the superintendent every few days for the duration of the fires."

The expanded public affairs staff spent a lot of time

dispelling the rumors and correcting the erroneous information that a long and crisis-oriented media event seems to generate. Everyone in the Service breathed a collective sigh of relief when the fires were finally extinguished. While the search for scapegoats began in political circles, Joan received kudos for her performance in directing the public affairs office during the long-running crisis. She is now the chief of Public Affairs for the National Park Service.

In normal times—if there are any normal times in a highly visible park like Yellowstone—what does a public affairs officer do? Typically, the public affairs officer is the official spokesperson for the park. Most large parks have a public affairs officer with a staff of two to four full-time employees and some part-time or seasonals working during the visitor season. In contrast, Everglades National Park in Florida, a large and popular park with plenty of media attention, is ably and solely served by Pat Tolle. In smaller parks, the interpretive division or the chief ranger handles public affairs functions.

In the larger parks, the public affairs officer is part of the management team and has the superintendent's backing in gathering information from the various divisions. To this end, Yellowstone has developed a fine-tuned emergency reporting center. Any incident—searches-and-rescues, fires, crimes, road or trail closings, injuries to visitors or park employees—is reported to the public affairs office. The park superintendent is kept informed, and the regional and Washington headquarters are notified of significant incidents.

As spokesperson, the public affairs officer represents and speaks for the superintendent. Speaking for the boss requires a thorough knowledge of management policies and the responsibilities of all divisions in order to answer questions and defuse potential controversies.

Public Affairs Officers

Pat Tolle's philosophy is to make her boss, the superintendent, look good. So far, she has been successful with six superintendents in her twenty years at Everglades.

One of the most important jobs of a public affairs officer is serving as the media contact for the park. Reporters seeking information contact the public affairs officer for details on a news story, quotes, the park's position in a controversy, and interviews with the superintendent. Whatever the situation, they often need immediate assistance. Successful public affairs officers maintain good relations with the media. "I know that many reporters are on a deadline," says Pat. "I've been at Everglades so long that I know right where to go to get the information they need." This type of response ensures good relations with the media.

Pat started in Everglades as the switchboard operator, where she learned all about the park. She then took a secretarial position before becoming an administrative assistant. Because of her knowledge of the park, she was asked to take over as the public affairs officer. Her history of good media relations provides the basis for a training course that she gives for Park Service employees.

Yellowstone and Everglades are both nationally and internationally known parks that usually generate news. Hardly a day goes by without a call from a major newspaper. The Yellowstone public affairs office responds to 2,000 media requests each year, fielding five to ten requests a day during an average week. If reporters come to the park, the public affairs officer arranges interviews and provides a guide, if needed. "We make sure they get what they want," says Pat. "We don't muzzle our employees, but we want our best, most articulate people to accompany reporters."

Both parks are favored by VIPs and high government

officials. Not surprisingly, Everglades is especially popular during the winter months. "I spend a lot of time making arrangements for VIP visits," remarks Pat. "Every author, videographer, and media celebrity wants to come to south Florida in January and February."

Among the VIPs who have visited Everglades in the past few years are President George Bush, Queen Elizabeth, the King of Norway, and Peter Jennings. Pat arranges for guides and crowd control and works with the rangers to set up an Incident Command System overhead team to handle emergency situations. When the President visited, she worked closely with the Secret Service to ensure his safety.

The VIPs usually avoid Yellowstone during the winter, but they arrive in force during the summer. Joan prepares itineraries for approximately 200 VIP visits each year. Yellowstone is renowned among foreign park officials, who visit frequently to observe various aspects of park management. If the Secretary of the Interior is visiting, Joan prepares an itinerary based on what he wants to see and do. The itinerary is finalized with the Secretary's public affairs office and his or her chief of staff. When the itinerary is set, Joan arranges for all aspects of the visit.

In addition to being a surrogate travel agent for the rich and famous, public affairs officers write press releases, speeches, and briefing papers. News such as the appointment of a new superintendent, special interpretive programs, criminal activity in the park, or special events are important to many communities around a park. The majority of parks are in rural areas, and while the announcement of a new superintendent at Yellowstone may get a paragraph in the *New York Times* or *Washington Post*, it is a major news story in towns around the park.

Occasionally a public affairs officer writes a speech

for a superintendent, although many write their own speeches and are good off-the-cuff speakers. The public affairs staffs in the regional and headquarters offices do more speech-writing because their management people usually speak to larger and more diverse interest groups and address topics with a broader regional or national perspective. The public affairs office in Washington may be asked to prepare a speech for the Secretary of the Interior to be given at a dedication ceremony in a park or at an annual meeting of a national conservation organization.

Briefing papers usually describe controversial situations and summarize the problem for the decision-makers. Problems and alternatives are framed in the briefing paper, enabling the top management people to make an informed decision. The Washington or regional offices may have twenty to twenty-five active issues and briefing papers at a given time.

When problems or controversies do arise in the park, the best strategy is to get out front with the Park Service story. "Always be first to announce a controversial story," advises Joan. "Don't ever try to suppress bad news or keep the press away, because the situation will eventually blow up and damage your credibility."

Recently a Yellowstone ranger shot a bear with a rubber bullet. He was trying to frighten the bear so it wouldn't return to populous areas. The bear was moving at the time, and the bullet penetrated the skin and killed it. Joan's reaction was to release the story immediately. Bears are a hot issue, because their numbers are declining and national conservation organizations are vocally interested in their welfare. The situation could have erupted had not the information been released quickly and accurately.

New York Times urban reporter David Dunlop agrees with this approach. Speaking at an Urban Superintendents Conference on ways to build a healthy relationship with the media, Dunlop told them, "Don't be willing to pitch the good news, then be unavailable when more compromising issues arise. Always level with reporters. Reporters come back again and again to someone who's leveled with them and been available in times of crisis." Dunlop went on to say, "If you deal candidly with reporters, you'll be rewarded with balanced media coverage of your park."

In her years of building good relations with the media, Pat Tolle has plotted this strategy from day one. "We have a lot of environmental problems at Everglades," she comments. "By going to the media first with the problem and explaining our side, we avoid playing catch-up and having to rebut each new story." Another bit of advice Pat offers in her media relations course is, "Avoid confrontations with the media. If you get crossways with reporters, you will be butchered in print."

Besides information requests from the media, there are numerous and often bizarre requests from the public. Phone and mail requests flood the public affairs office, especially after major magazine articles. The Park Service headquarters information office in the Interior Building gets hit the hardest. It annually receives some 33,000 mail requests and 25,000 phone requests, in addition to 5,400 visitors who stop in to pick up maps or ask for advice. Not all requests are easy to answer. One person confused national parks with amusement parks and wrote to express his displeasure at finding no roller coaster in Rocky Mountain National Park.

Requests for commercial film permits are approved in the public affairs office. Yellowstone receives an average of 200 film requests each year but issues only forty to fifty permits. Approval depends on the amount of disruption the filming will cause. Will it disrupt park operations? Will it interfere with visitors or impact the wildlife? The overriding goal is to protect the resources and provide services to the public. "If a crew wants to film Old Faithful from the air and it means helicopters buzzing the area all day during the height of the tourist season, we'll deny the permit," explains Joan. "That may be the only opportunity some of our visitors have to see Old Faithful, and we don't want it ruined for them."

Public affairs offices handle Freedom of Information Act (FOIA) requests, which allow access to Park Service files. Unless the file is classified "secret," the public can use the information for a nominal reproduction fee.

Regional and headquarters offices work closely with national tourism organizations to promote the national parks. The individual parks are concerned with state and local tourism. Many parks are vital to the regional economy. The regional economy of Yellowstone was hurt by the fires of 1988, but it has boomed since then, with more visitors coming to see the after effects of the fires. In the past, West Yellowstone has resembled a ghost town after Labor Day; since 1989, however, the town is busy through September.

Joan is the park's liaison with the tourism industry, and she works extensively with state and local tourist officials. She also works with the other park divisions on construction project information to minimize disruptions to the tourist economy. During road construction projects, she tries to ensure that visitors are not completely routed away from the nearby tourism-dependent towns.

Fact checking of publications is another function of the public affairs office. Proposed articles in national magazines and travel guides are checked for accuracy, corrected if necessary, and returned to the publisher. Publishers and authors also request photographs and slides through the public affairs office. Large photo and slide collections are available at the headquarters and regional offices.

Deftly handling all these responsibilities requires special skills. Unfortunately, there are few ways for Park Service employees to learn these skills other than jumping right in. "We need training courses in public affairs, and we need to expand the profession and provide a career with upward mobility to attract people to it," Joan says. "Public affairs is a growing field, and more of our employees need to acquire the skills. There is no career ladder for public affairs, and there should be!"

Pat Tolle echoes Joan's comments about the need for training opportunities and a career ladder. In the meantime, she offers this bit of advice to people who think they would be interested in public affairs positions: "Seek opportunities to work with the media in any capacity. Only by working with them can you develop an understanding of their role and operating techniques and how to communicate effectively with and through them."

Joan recommends that anyone interested in a public affairs career develop strong communication skills. Speaking and writing skills are essential. You have to be able to articulate your information clearly both by speaking and by writing. The cliché "being able to think on your feet" also applies. The media may be peppering you with questions and you need to respond quickly and accurately. You have to be flexible, adapt to rapid changes in a situation, and be able to handle the pressure of several emergencies at the same time. Joan recalls a fatal plane crash in Yellowstone Lake at the same time a fire was starting and a man had fallen into the Grand Canyon of the Yellowstone River.

You need basic people skills for dealing with the everyday visitor, and diplomatic skills for working with high-level officials from the park to the Department of the Interior and sometimes even the White House. If meeting deadlines gives you heartburn, look for another career; you may have only fifteen minutes to summarize a controversy and provide the park's response. The job demands that you remain cool and calm at all times. The wide variety of situations and the people you meet guarantee a lively and interesting career where you're always at the center of the action.

19

Concessions Specialists

It may surprise you to learn that the clerk at the El Tovar Hotel desk in Grand Canyon National Park is not a Park Service employee. Neither is the waitress in the hotel restaurant nor the driver of the tour bus along the Canyon rim. These people and thousands of others are employed by private businesses known as concessions, which provide services to the public in the national parks. Services in the form of hotels, restaurants, souvenir shops, bus and boat tours, gas stations, saddle horses, whitewater raft trips, and more are available to visitors through business arrangements between the Park Service and concessioners.

The legislation creating the National Park Service in 1916 provided the basic authority for park concessions. The Service was given the dual mission of safeguarding the parks' resource values and providing for visitor enjoyment. Finding the proper balance between the two missions is not always easy. Concessions have grown in the parks to the point where today's concessioners gross over $600 million in sales and vary in size from small owner-operated facilities to multimillion-dollar corporations.

Working with the concessioners to insure quality facilities and experiences for the visitors are the Park Service concessions management specialists. The organization has 322 concessions positions, of which 102 are full-time professionals. The remaining 220 are park employees who are responsible for concessions management as a collateral duty.

Because the work of a concessions specialist is totally involved with the private industry (concessioners), a background in business, hotel/restaurant management, law, commercial appraisal, or accounting is necessary. Grades in the full-time positions are usually above the GS-9 level, but the collateral-duty positions are often assigned to rangers whose grade level is normally below the GS-9. Every park with a concession operation has at least one person assigned to concessions management as a collateral duty. Some parks have a full-time concessions specialist, and the largest parks like Grand Canyon or Yosemite have a concessions division of four to six employees.

The regional and Washington offices also have concessions divisions to provide direction and assistance to the parks. The Washington office develops concessions management policy and training programs and is responsible for determining the franchise fees. The regional offices guide the parks in following the policies and draft contracts with the concessioners.

The General Management Plan (GMP) determines the kind and number of services needed in a park. Concessions are limited to those considered necessary for visitors' enjoyment, and the concession must be an appropriate match for the purposes of the park. Working with the GMP, the concessions specialists develop a prospectus seeking private industry to provide those services. The prospectus clearly states the type and quantity of the service to be provided, the location and size of any construction, the investment required, and the franchise fee.

The Park Service initiates concession proposals. They do not accept unsolicited business proposals, and

Concessions Specialists

they introduce a proposal only after a need is identified and the park resources are deemed safe from any development.

Concession specialists then draft and negotiate the contract with the concessioner and approve the rates to be charged. Contract drafting and negotiation are usually done by the regional office concession specialists, although at a large park the concessions specialists negotiate contracts. Rate approval is based on a comparability study, which analyzes prices charged by similar companies operating in a competitive situation. Park Service concessioners are without competition in the park. The proper term is "regulated monopoly," much like a public utility. If left unregulated, they could take advantage of their position and charge prices up to what the market would bear. Through the comparability studies, the concessions specialist ensures that prices are comparable to those outside the park, while also allowing for a wide range of services and prices to provide the visitor a choice.

The concessions specialists in the parks review and evaluate the concessioners' performance each year for cleanliness, service, and quality. Are they following health and safety guidelines? Are they properly insured? Have they completed their construction program? Have they submitted their annual financial report? The specialist evaluates all this according to certain standards developed for twenty-five different services. Formal site inspections are made one to four times a year.

Based on these reviews, concessioners receive an annual rating of satisfactory, marginal, or unsatisfactory. If a concessioner receives a marginal or unsatisfactory rating, the park or regional specialists work with the concessioner to improve the deficiencies. A contract can be terminated with an unsatisfactory rating, but that is rarely necessary.

Old Faithful Inn at Yellowstone National Park, one of the many facilities operated by concessioners (National Park Service).

Bruce Wadlington is the chief of concessions management at Grand Canyon National Park, where he supervises a staff of four and works with twenty-eight concessioners. "We maintain a good but businesslike relationship with the concessioners," says Bruce. "It is unlikely that concessioners will be terminated, because they usually have a large investment in their business. They take pride in their operation and are willing to make changes when necessary to correct deficiencies."

Fred Suarez, a concessions specialist in the Midwest Regional Office in Omaha, Nebraska, agrees with Bruce's assessment. "If the review shows that concessioners are not fulfilling their contracts, we try to work with them to improve their services. We want concessioners to be successful because the visitors need their services. We only terminate contracts if they won't improve."

The rate comparability studies and the evaluations were started in the early 1980s and comprise a major part of the workload for a park concessions specialist. But the work is effective. In the 1970s the Washington office received 200 to 300 complaints each year. In 1994 more than 269 million visitors came to the parks, but only 29 complaints came to Washington.

The specialists also collect the annual franchise fee from the concessioner, ensure that the proper percentage of receipts is paid, and review the required annual financial reports. Most of the large concessioners are able to run a profitable business. Figures for 1993 show that 83 concessioners had gross receipts over $1 million. For struggling concessioners, the park and regional specialists analyze the financial reports and work with them to improve their business. Concessions specialists with a business background are helpful in suggesting operating changes, and they are knowledgeable about similar businesses that are successful in other parks. Everyone benefits from a thriving, well-run concession: the concessioner, the Park Service, and the visitor.

20

Training

Throughout your Park Service career, training will be available in your career field or specialty. You may even rise to such eminence in your field that the Park Service asks you to train other employees.

The employees are the Park Service's greatest resource. Think about your visits to the national parks and watching the rangers at their jobs. What impressed you? Was it the energized presentation of an interpretive ranger as he placed you in the front lines at Gettysburg, or was it the quiet competence of the law enforcement ranger as she sorted out a traffic accident, took command of the situation, administered first aid to the injured, and got traffic flowing again? Were you impressed by the general cheerfulness and helpfulness of park employees as they answered your questions and guided you along? Was it a contact with a ranger that sparked your interest in working for the Park Service?

Park Service employees are the organization's best ambassadors. Recognizing that people are the key to success, the Service offers general and specialized training for employees to continue the development of their skills and careers.

Courses are offered at the national, regional, and park levels. Typically about ninety courses are offered nationally, and anyone in the Park Service can attend. Regional courses are available to employees in a specific

Park Service region. One year a region had a large number of new superintendents, and training courses in administration, personnel management, and cultural/natural resources were presented to help these first-timers navigate their course in running a park. Park-level courses address the needs of the park and utilize local experts. Computer training is usually offered at the park level to bring all employees to a standard level of computer competence. Examples of other park-level courses are "Substance Abuse Awareness" and "Coping with Stress."

Examples of courses offered nationally are "Orientation to NPS Operations," a week-long course to familiarize new employees with the overall mission and operation of the Service; "Ranger Skills," a six-week course designed to demonstrate the essential skills that rangers must have and to introduce them to all the programs such as interpretation, law enforcement, resource management, maintenance, supervision, and administration; "Historic Preservation Maintenance Skills Workshop," a two-week hands-on course teaching maintenance staffs how to maintain and preserve historic structures; and "Natural Resources for Superintendents," a week-long introduction to natural resources for those who have had minimal experience.

When a deficiency or need is identified, the Park Service develops courses to fill that particular vacuum. In the early 1980s, resource management "arrived." Before then, the rangers did resource management work on an as-needed basis. Then the 1980 *Threats to the Parks Report* to Congress detailed the ongoing and potential natural and cultural resource degradation occurring in the parks caused by development activities outside the parks. Reviewing the thousands of documented threats to resources, Park Service management realized that rangers were stretched too thin and a specialist in resource management was needed.

Thus was born the first resource management trainee class in 1982, consisting of thirty-three employees who completed two years of intensive training in biological sciences and cultural resource courses while working in the parks. On completion of the program, the Park Service had thirty-three resource managers. The program continues today as a one-year course.

The courses are taught by employees of the Park Service and other federal agencies who are experts in their field. Experts from the private sector are often utilized. Most courses are taught at the Park Service Training Centers in Harpers Ferry, West Virginia, and Grand Canyon, Arizona. The Federal Law Enforcement Training center (FLETC) in Glynco, Georgia, develops the law-enforcement courses. Two other training centers are the Williamsport Preservation Training Center (WPTC) in Williamsport, Maryland, and the Boise Interagency Fire Center (BIFC) in Boise, Idaho. WPTC is devoted exclusively to developing specialists who can both perform and direct preservation work on the thousands of historic structures in the National Park System. The Boise Fire Center consists of six federal agencies working together to manage wildfires on range and forested lands. Fire training is developed there and presented onsite and at other locations across the country.

Each training facility has a superintendent and a small staff. The staff is responsible for scheduling courses, arranging for instructors, and insuring that everything runs smoothly during the course. They also serve as instructors and are responsible for developing new training courses as the need arises.

Dale Ditmanson, superintendent at Florissant Fossil

Beds in Colorado, spent three years at Harpers Ferry Center as a training specialist. The job was a bit different from what Dale had expected. "I assumed that 40 to 50 percent of my time would be spent as a classroom instructor, and in the remaining time I would be working with the program managers in the Washington headquarters office to develop new courses," said Dale. "Instead, only 20 percent of my time was in the classroom. Developing new courses and program coordination took up most of my day."

New courses are usually suggested by program managers in Washington. As an example, the resource management staff may identify a need for Wilderness Area Management training. Working within its annual training budget, the NPS Employee Development Division in Washington sets priorities for the coming year. If the Wilderness course is selected, Dale starts working with the resource management specialists in Washington to develop the course objectives and content. Each course features different teaching methods and a variety of speakers. Usually the program managers suggest instructors, because they work with wilderness use experts or know by reputation the leaders in the wilderness field.

Training specialists rarely get a break. As Dale describes it, "The schedule was hectic. While I had one course going on, I was lining up speakers for courses six weeks away and writing announcements for others that were three months away. And then I was developing classroom materials for every class."

Despite the frenzied schedules and the heartburn of running a course when the speakers are late or don't show, the job does have its rewards. 'I received an international assignment to help develop an interpretive program for rangers in Thailand," Dale explained. "The International Affairs Division arranged for me to travel to Thailand's national parks and work with their rangers. I also worked on a variety of courses such as interpretation, acid rain, archeology, and remote areas management so that I was able to pick up pieces of information from all the courses.

"The most enjoyable aspect of the job was the exposure to the people who manage and run the Park Service. The Mather Training Center is a little over an hours' drive from Washington, so we were able to recruit the top policy makers and program managers as instructors."

These staff positions are often stepping-stones to additional job opportunities in your career. Training center staffers meet a tremendous number of people in just one year. They meet the trainees and the trainers, many of whom are superintendents or management people from the central or regional office. Such contacts can only help your career, and most of the training center staffers move on to better jobs in the Park Service.

21

Seasonal Employment

Each year millions of people from the United States and abroad flood the national parks. To help serve these visitors and protect the park resources, the Park Service hires a large seasonal work force to augment the permanent staff.

Seasonal employees outnumber full-time employees in the Park Service. Like Volunteers in Parks (Chapter 22), seasonals can do any job that the rangers do. Unlike the volunteers, however, the seasonals are paid for their labor and those with law-enforcement commissions can perform front-line law-enforcement functions.

Summertime, June through August, when visitation is heaviest, is when seasonals are most needed. Besides working in the parks, seasonals are also needed in the headquarters office in Washington and at the ten regional offices around the country.

The positions available every year include law-enforcement rangers, tour guides, naturalists, firefighters, laborers, fee collectors, historians, lifeguards, backcountry rangers, clerk/typists, carpenters, and many more. Whatever the job, seasonal employees have the opportunity to learn more about the National Park Service and its mission. More important, seasonals acquire valuable experience and learn about opportunities for permanent employment.

Despite the annual need for so many people, these jobs are very difficult to get. Every year the number of applicants far outnumbers the positions available. Newcomers are competing against experienced seasonal employees. Teachers fill many positions, being usually available for ten to twelve weeks during the summer. My friend Max Miller taught high school math in Midland, Texas, for sixteen years and spent every summer as a backcountry ranger at Rocky Mountain National Park in Colorado.

In addition to the competition and large number of applicants, federal regulations require that veterans be given preference among applicants. Despite these discouraging words, there are excellent opportunities for anyone with law-enforcement experience or training. Also competition is less keen during the winter season and at the smaller parks.

Parks that need winter seasonals include Everglades, Death Valley, Joshua Tree, and the Virgin Islands. During the summer season, everyone wants to work at Yellowstone, Grand Teton, Rocky Mountain, and Yosemite. Try applying at parks like St. Croix National Wild and Scenic River along the Minnesota/Wisconsin border or Sleeping Bear Dunes National Lakeshore on Michigan's west coast, both in beautiful scenic areas. The Park Service has published a booklet entitled, "The National Parks: Lesser Known Areas." You can get a free copy by writing to the public information office at any of the NPS regional offices or the headquarters office.

The entry-level grades for seasonal positions range from GS-2 to GS-4. (See Appendix 3 for an explanation of GS grades.) The standard workweek is 40 hours. Most seasonal park rangers and maintenance people are required to wear the NPS uniform; the Service partly subsidizes uniform purchase. Hous-

Seasonal Employment

ing may be available for seasonals, but don't count on it.

For application forms and additional information on seasonal employment, write to: National Park Service, Seasonal Employment Unit, P.O. Box 37127, Washington, DC 20013-7127. For summer seasonal positions, applications are taken between September 1 and (postmarked by) January 15. The application period for winter seasonal employment is June 1 through (postmarked by) July 15.

Another seasonal employment opportunity in the parks is at the hotels, lodges, restaurants, stores, marinas, and other visitor facilities operated by concessioners. These concessioners recruit, hire, and train their own employees and usually pay minimum wage. The majority of concessioner jobs are filled by high school and college students. Some of the large concession operations provide housing for their employees in the form of cabins or a dormitory. If you saw the movie "Dirty Dancing," the scenes of the employees' cabins (and after-work parties) are similar to a large concession operation.

If you are interested in working for a concessioner, write the park where you want to work and request the names and addresses of its concessioners. Another source of information is: Conference of National Park Concessioners, c/o G.B. Hanson, Mammoth Cave, KY 42259; phone: (502) 773-2191. This organization publishes a book entitled, *National Parks Visitor Facilities and Services*, which lists the parks that have concession operations, describes the facilities, and provides addresses and phone numbers. The book can be purchased from the above address for $4.50 postpaid. Write directly to the concessioner for job applications and information on job availability, wages, and working and living conditions.

22

Volunteers in Parks (VIPs)

Volunteers in Parks, or VIPs, are like volunteers everywhere in that they work without pay. However, the national parks are special places to work, and each year thousands of citizens volunteer their time and talents to ensure that our parks will be enjoyed by future generations.

In a typical park, there is more work than the staff can accomplish, and budget cutbacks throughout the federal government prevent the hiring of new staff. Roy Graybill, national coordinator for the Volunteers in Parks program, says, "Volunteers are essential to the Park Service. We can't get all the work done. If the volunteers didn't do it, it wouldn't get done." In 1991 the Park Service benefited from the work of 75,000 volunteers, who accomplished an estimated $35 million worth of work.

Working as a VIP is a way to sample a career in the Park Service. VIPs are a diverse group ranging from high school and college students to teachers, scientists, artists, lawyers, farmers, and retirees. Each volunteer brings a needed talent or skill to the park. The goal of the VIP program is to use this voluntary help in a way that benefits the volunteer and the Park Service. The minimum age for VIPs is eighteen, although persons under eighteen can become VIPs in their home community with permission from their parent or guardian.

What do VIPs do in the parks? According to Graybill, "Any work that Park Service employees do, the volunteers can do. The only exception is front-line law enforcement, which is left to park rangers." Below is a sampling of the jobs that volunteers do:

- Work at an information desk answering visitors' questions and handing out written information.
- Write or design visitor brochures.
- Answer telephone and mail requests.
- Prepare and conduct special park events.
- Maintain trails.
- Build fences, paint buildings, and make cabinets.
- Serve as a campground host.
- Present living history demonstrations in period costume.
- Pick up litter along roads, seashores, trails, and rivers.
- Patrol trails on foot or on horseback.
- Assist with the preservation and treatment of museum artifacts.
- Take photographs.
- Demonstrate arts and crafts.
- Assist resource managers and researchers by making wildlife counts, planting trees, etc.
- Design computer programs for park use.

When you are selected as a VIP, you are given training to acquaint you with the specific duties of your job and with the park. You may work a few hours a week or month, seasonally, or full time, weekdays, weekends, day or night. Whenever you are available, the park will try to accommodate you.

To apply for a VIP position, write or call the VIP coordinator at the national park where you would like to volunteer and request an application. You can apply to

Volunteers in Parks (VIPs)

more than one park. Each park is a local operation with recruiting, selection, and training handled on site. To obtain a park address, write or call the appropriate National Park Service regional office (see Appendix 1).

If you don't live near a national park, contact the Student Conservation Association (SCA). The SCA is the largest single provider of full-time volunteers to assist federal and state natural resource management agencies. The majority of high school students working in the parks are supplied by the SCA.

In addition to the National Park Service, the SCA also provides volunteers to the U.S. Forest Service, the U.S. Fish and Wildlife Service, the Bureau of Land Management, the U.S. Navy, and on state and private lands. There are two programs for volunteers, the High School Program and the Resource Assistant Program. Each year the SCA places more than 450 high school students and 1,000 adult volunteers in its programs.

The High School Program brings together students from throughout the United States and puts them in work crews of six to ten directed by experienced SCA leaders. For four or five weeks these groups live, work, and play in national parks, national forests, or remote wilderness areas. Housing is a rustic tent camp. Projects range from trail construction and maintenance to bridge construction or site revegetation and restoration.

There is no charge for this program. Students provide the labor and SCA provides leadership, food, and group camping gear. Students are responsible for their travel to the program area. Following completion of their project, each group goes on a week-long backpacking or canoe trip.

The Resource Assistant Program is for college students and adults and places volunteers with land management agencies for twelve to sixteen weeks of intensive training and service alongside professional

A Student Conservation Association (SCA) crew of New York City high school students doing trail maintenance at Acadia National Park in Maine (SCA photo).

rangers, foresters, resource managers, scientists, and other environmental specialists. Resource Assistants help the professional staff with wildlife research projects involving mammal and bird surveys and backcountry trail patrol and provide visitor information and educational programs. These jobs often entail extensive fieldwork. Many participants use the Resource Assistant Program as a way to sample a career in the outdoors.

Unlike the High School Program, those in the Resource Assistant Program are provided with travel and food expenses plus free housing. Both programs are funded jointly by the SCA and the areas that offer

Volunteers in Parks (VIPs)

positions. SCA raises money through tax-deductible contributions from individuals, foundations, and corporations.

For more information, contact Student Conservation Association, P.O. Box 550, Charlestown, NH, 03603-0550; phone: (603) 543-1700.

23

Applying for a Federal Government Job

If you decide to try for a job with the National Park Service or with any federal government agency, your first stop should be your local Office of Personnel Management (OPM), to find out what is available and how to apply. The OPM offices across the country also house the Federal Job Information Centers (FJIC) discussed below.

Federal agencies fill job vacancies in several ways. They may promote an employee into the vacancy, reinstate a former employee, or hire an applicant from another agency. They also may request the names of applicants from an OPM register or obtain direct hiring authority from OPM. For some positions, you can apply directly to the Park Service, whereas others require you to get on an OPM List of Eligibles, or pass an examination, or both. The best source of information about a job is the examination announcement. It explains the jobs covered by the exam, what experience is required, what the jobs pay, and how to apply. Your experience, interest, and education can guide you in deciding which announcement covers the job you want, or an Information Specialist at your nearby FJIC can help you.

Generally, with a bachelor's degree you can qualify

for entry-level positions in grades 5/7, but you have to take an exam and get a rating from OPM.

You can apply for most jobs with a résumé or an application form known as OF-612, the Optional Application for Federal Employment. The job announcement will require certain specific information but for every job your résumé or application form must provide the following information:

Job Information
The announcement number, title, and grade(s) of the job.

Personal Information
Full name and mailing address with zip code and phone numbers and Social Security Number.
   Country of citzenship (most federal jobs require U.S. citizenship).

Education
High School—name, city, state; date of diploma or GED Colleges—name, city, state; majors; type and year of any degrees received.

Work Experience
Provide information for your paid and unpaid work experience related to the job for which you are applying. Include: job title; duties and accomplishments; employer's name and address; supervisor's name and phone number; starting and ending dates (month and year); hours per week; salary.

Other Qualifications
Job-related training courses (title and year); job-related skills such as other languages, computers, machinery, typing; job-related honors, awards, and special accom-

plishments; memberships in professional or honor societies; leadership and public speaking activities.

Even if you have very little experience for the job for which you are applying, fill in your employment history as completely as possible. My first federal job was with the U.S. Army Corps of Engineers in Fort Worth, Texas, as an outdoor recreation planner. I applied for the job while I was in graduate school and was hired upon finishing my coursework. My previous work experience had been on construction crews building roads in Michigan, jobs that required brawn but not much in the way of brains. I had no experience at all in my new job although my college courses had been geared toward a career in natural resources work. My boss knew I lacked practical experience, so he paired me with one of the senior planners. The boss remarked that although there were many applicants for the job, he selected me because I had filled the application with previous jobs I had held. He said it didn't matter that I lacked experience for this job (it was an entry-level position) because my application showed that I had always worked when I wasn't in school and he'd rather take a chance on someone who showed a willingness to work. So my advice is to take your time and do a thorough and complete job with your resume or application.

Back to OPM. Periodically, OPM announces job openings. Some announcements are open for a limited time; others are open until all the vacancies are filled. You may have to take an examination to qualify for the job. When you apply for OPM-announced positions, applications are accepted only for the listed positions, grade levels, and work locations. If you apply for a landscape architect position but there are no openings at the time, you'll get your application back.

Assuming you've applied for an announced position, OPM reviews your application and mails you a "Notice of

Results." This identifies the jobs and grade levels for which you qualify, your test scores if an exam was required, the geographic areas where you are eligible, and how long your name will remain on the register for referral to a federal agency for their job openings. You have to keep your eligibility current, or your name is removed from the register.

Honorably discharged veterans receive an advantage known as veteran preference. Veteran preference adds five or ten points to a person's eligibility score, which determines the order of names on an OPM register. Veterans applying for federal jobs should check with their FJIC about this and other benefits that may apply to their situation.

When a park unit, a regional office, or the Washington office has a vacancy, one of the ways they can fill the position is by asking OPM for a list of eligibles. OPM forwards the names and applications of the best qualified candidates to the Park Service.

Don't be discouraged thinking that your name will be lost among the millions on the register. The process works despite the impression that your name is the proverbial needle in the haystack. Three landscape architects with whom I worked on various planning teams were hired from the register. I can't stress this enough: Visit or call your local FJIC, talk to an Information Specialist, and find out what steps you must take to get on the appropriate register.

The federal government has a program, Administrative Careers With America (ACWA), that offers the opportunity to compete for one of the thousands of entry-level positions available. Entry-level positions start at the GS-5 or GS-7 grade level. The program fills positions in nearly 100 occupations through one of two options: a written exam, or an application based on grade point average (GPA). Written exams are offered in six occupational groups. Based on the exam score, your name is placed on a list of eligible applicants and referred to federal agencies when they request candidates for vacancies.

The second option allows you to be hired directly by a federal agency based on your GPA/scholastic record. I prefer this option because you don't have to take an exam and you are applying for a specific vacancy. To qualify, you must have a GPA of 3.5 or higher (based on the 4.0 scale) for all undergraduate work or have graduated in the upper 10 percent of your class.

Several other entry-level positions in the ACWA program do not require a written test but completion of specific college coursework. These positions include: archeology, economics, anthropology, geography, history, museum management (curator), archivist, sociology, community planning, and foreign affairs. Applications are submitted to the local OPM Area Office only when it announces a specific vacancy.

OPM has a 24-hour job information hotline: (912)757-3000. For a listing of the statewide FJIC offices, a booklet on Administrative Careers with America, and a brochure entitled "Applying for a Federal Job" write: United States Office of Personnel Management, Washington, DC 20415.

24

Career Tips

The following tips, collected from Park Service employees, will help you get that first job with the Park Service and advance in your career.

1. Volunteer to work at a national park or even a state or local park. The experience, especially if you give tours or interpretive presentations, will give you an edge toward seasonal employment with the Park Service.
2. Try to get a summer job in a park. You'll be exposed to how a park operates and what each employee's role is. It may help you determine whether you want a career in the national parks and if so, what career.
3. Start exploring the possibility of summer work at least one year in advance. All seasonal employment applications go to the Seasonal Employment Unit in Washington, D.C., no matter what park you want to work in. The summer season recruitment period is September 1 through January 15; the winter period, June 1 through July 15. Applications postmarked after the closing date are not accepted. For an information packet and application forms, write to: National Park Service, Sea-

sonal Employment Unit, P.O. Box 37127, Washington, DC 20013-7127.
4. If you can't get a summer job with the Park Service, apply for a job with a concessioner, private businesses that provide lodging, food, and other services such as pack horse trips, boat/raft trips, and various sightseeing trips. They constantly need dependable, responsible summer help. Many concessioners provide lodging and meals as part of the employment package. Contact the park where you want to work for the names and addresses of their concessioners, or the Conference of National Park Concessioners, Mammoth Cave, KY, 42259; phone: (502) 773-2191.
5. Another option is to try for a seasonal position with another federal agency such as the Bureau of Land Management, Fish & Wildlife Service, or the Forest Service. Previous federal employment always looks good when you apply for a permanent position.
6. Go to one of the seasonal (200 hours) law-enforcement training sessions offered by universities around the country (see Appendix 2). A seasonal law-enforcement commission makes a potential candidate much more attractive for seasonal or permanent employment.
7. To get started in the Park Service, you may have to accept a position at a large urban park such as Gateway National Recreation Area in the New York City area, Independence National Historical Park in Philadelphia, Jefferson National Expansion Memorial in St. Louis, or Golden Gate National Recreation Area in San Francisco. At the entry-level posi-

tions, these expensive areas may strain your finances, with or without a family. But accept the jobs if you can afford it, because you'll be in the Service as a permanent full-time employee (after a standard probationary period). Once you're employed by the Park Service, you can compete for other vacancies as they occur around the country.

8. Getting into the Park Service is the hard part. If necessary, accept a job as a clerk-typist even if you are qualified for a professional position. Once in the organization, you can apply for the available professional positions. I know of a biologist with a master's degree who hired on as a GS-3 clerk-typist and was able to land a GS-9 resource management position eight months later. OPM has a clerical examination that allows the Park Service to hire a person directly from a list of eligibles without competition at the GS-4 level.

9. Once in the Park Service, acquire as many skills as you can and take as much specialized training as possible. Skills such as public speaking can be developed through practice and organizations like Toastmasters International. Specialized training in firefighting, interpretive skills, or wilderness management will increase your knowledge and enhance your desirability for future vacancies. Training is offered through various Park Service courses at the Albright Training Center at Grand Canyon in Arizona or at the Mather Training Center in Harpers Ferry, West Virginia. Other federal and state agencies provide training that is open to Park Service employees. Each regional office has an employee development of-

fice and a training officer who can help you find the type of training that you need.
10. Take the initiative in seeking out career development opportunities. In the Park Service they range from informal assignments to additional education and training, but you have to find them. Take charge of your own career.
11. Be mobile. Once you have a permanent job in the Park Service, you can advance your career through willingness to move around within the System. Often such moves involve a promotion, as the new job may require increased responsibilities or supervisory responsibilities.

Walt Dabney, the former chief ranger of the National Park Service, worked in Yellowstone National Park as a naturalist the summer before his senior year at Texas A&M University. After graduating, he began as an interpreter in the Harpers Ferry Training Center in West Virginia, then moved to a ranger position at Yosemite, where he was promoted to district ranger. Walt then moved to Mount Rainier National Park, Washington, as a district ranger and from there to Grand Teton National Park, Wyoming, as a law enforcement specialist. The next stop was Everglades National Park, Florida, as chief of resource management before moving to headquarters in Washington as the chief ranger of the Service. From Washington, he went on to his present position as superintendent of Canyonlands and Arches National Parks in Utah.

Notice that along Walt's career path, he moved into jobs with different responsibilities to broaden his knowledge of park operations.

Career Tips

This variety of responsibilities also increased his ability to compete for other job openings.
12. If you want to advance to managerial positions, sometime during your NPS career you'll have to work in a regional office or the Washington office. Working in these congested urban areas is distasteful to many NPS people, but if you can put in at least three years, the experience will be invaluable to your career.

    Working in a park, your concerns are for the care and preservation of that specific park. In a regional office, you enlarge your concerns to encompass all the parks in your multistate region. Working in the headquarters office in Washington, however, your concerns are on a national level and your perspective broadens.

    Washington experience is especially important because it is the place where policies and decisions are made for the entire system. You may deal with members of Congress and their staffs and make important contacts. You will spend much of your time helping the regional offices and individual parks solve problems. You'll see how laws are created, passed, and implemented and observe how the Park Service operates on a national level. The Washington office is an exciting place to work, and the experience will benefit you as you return to the field in a managerial position.
13. You've just started with the Park Service as a permanent employee. What's your next step? Try to develop a career plan and goals for yourself. Where do you want to be five, ten, fifteen, and twenty years from now? If you

have an idea of where you want to be—park superintendent, resource manager of a large park, regional director—you can guide your career to the jobs and contacts that will get you there. In the Introduction, I mentioned Bill Supernaugh's goal of being superintendent at Joshua Tree National Monument, where his father had been superintendent. Bill graduated from Humboldt State University in California with a degree in wildlife biology and became a ranger. Like Walt Dabney, he moved around the country, taking positions with more responsibility and visibility. He has worked in both the Philadelphia regional office and the Washington headquarters office, and he was the Park Service representative at the Federal Law Enforcement Training Facility (FLETC) in Glynco, Georgia. He is now assistant superintendent at Indiana Dunes National Lakeshore. The expression, "He's had all his tickets punched," applies to Bill, and he is well qualified for a superintendency, possibly at Joshua Tree.

14. Learn the budget process. No matter where you work, the funding level of your position or program determines what can be accomplished. Budgets are like gas for a car: They provide the fuel for programs.

Ask your supervisor how your program budget works and how it relates to the overall park budget. Then follow the process on up the line where the park's budget goes to the regional office and the regional offices submit their budgets to headquarters in Washington. Ask how budget decisions are made at each level: park, regional, and national. The more you

Career Tips

learn about how the budget is formulated and finalized, the better will be your grasp of how a park operates.

Here is a simplified example of a fictional park's budget. Brandy Station National Historical Park in Virginia commemorates a Civil War cavalry battle and has an annual budget of $1,000,000. Four park divisions share in this money. The Maintenance Division uses $400,000, Resource Management and Visitor Protection (RM&VP) uses $300,000, Interpretation uses $200,000, and Administration uses $100,000. Interest in the Civil War is increasing, and the park is hosting more visitors each year.

Each division needs to expand to keep up with visitor needs. Maintenance is requesting $50,000 more for trail upkeep and restroom cleaning. The RM&VP Division wants to hire two additional rangers, for which they need $60,000. They also need an additional $50,000 for vegetation studies and one biologist. Interpretation wants $100,000 to hire three additional rangers and develop a self-guided cassette tape tour of the park. Administration needs $90,000 to computerize recordkeeping. In all, $350,000 more. The Regional Office has instructed the superintendent of Brandy Station that he may apply for budget increases up to $75,000, but there is no guarantee that the park will receive one penny more than the budget of $1,000,000.

The superintendent must decide on his top priority for the $75,000. He decides that one seasonal ranger and one biologist for the RM&VP division and one interpretive ranger are most important. He submits a budget request for $1,075,000. The regional office prioritizes the requests of all the parks in the region and decides which increases to approve based on how much money the region is allocated by the Washington office.

As mentioned, this is a simplified version of the process. Other factors enter into it, such as whether or not the region can hire more rangers, what are the top national and regional priorities this year, etc. Learn as much as you can about the whole process. There are no particular courses that will help you prepare a budget at the program level. If you enjoy budget work and want to do it full time, courses in business and finance are beneficial.

15. Certain jobs have high visibility and often come into contact with top management people in the regional and headquarters offices. Working as a training officer at one of the two training centers involves contact with the superintendents and policy makers. You can scope out the high-visibility jobs and see if they are something you are qualified to do and would like to do.

16. If your goal is to be a supervisor, learn something from every one of your supervisors to prepare yourself for your day. Learn from the good ones. Why are they effective? Why are they respected? How do they treat people? You can even learn from an incompetent supervisor—techniques or styles to avoid. Retain the good, discard the bad, but keep learning.

Appendix 1
National Park Service Regional Offices

Northeast Field Area
National Park Service
U.S. Customs House
200 Chestnut Street, Room 306
Philadelphia, PA 19106
(215) 597-7013
Jurisdiction:
Maine, New Hampshire, Vermont, Rhode Island, Massachusetts, Connecticut, New York, Pennsylvania, New Jersey, Virginia, West Virginia, Maryland, Delaware.

National Capital Field Area
National Park Service
1100 Ohio Drive SW
Washington, DC 20242
(202) 619-7005
Jurisdiction:
Washington DC, and some parks in Maryland, Virginia, and West Virginia.

Southeast Field Area
National Park Service
75 Spring Street SW
Atlanta, GA 30303

Appendix 1

(404) 331-4916
Jurisdiction:
Kentucky, Tennessee, North Carolina, South Carolina, Georgia, Florida, Alabama, Mississippi, Louisiana, Puerto Rico, Virgin Islands.

Midwest Field Area
National Park Service
1709 Jackson Street
Omaha, NE 68102
(402) 221-3431
Jurisdiction:
Michigan, Ohio, Indiana, Illinois, Wisconsin, Minnesota, Iowa, Missouri, Arkansas, Kansas, Nebraska, North Dakota, South Dakota.

International Field Area
National Park Service
P.O. Box 25287
Denver, CO 80225-0287
(303) 969-2500
Jurisdiction:
Oklahoma, Texas, New Mexico, Arizona, Utah, Colorado, Wyoming, Montana.

Pacific West Field Area
National Park Area
600 Harrison Street, Suite 600
San Francisco, CA 94107-1372
(415) 744-3955
Jurisdiction:
Washington, Oregon, Idaho, California, Nevada, Hawaii, Guam.

APPENDIX 1

Alaska Field Area
National Park Service
2525 Gambell Street, Room 107
Anchorage, AK 99503-2892
(907) 257-2570
Jurisdiction:
All Alaska parks.

Appendix 2
Seasonal Law Enforcement Training Program Schools

NOTE: This list is subject to change. For current listings contact: National Park Service, Seasonal Law Enforcement Training Program, Federal Law Enforcement Training Center, Building 64, Room 219, Glynco, GA 31524

University of Alaska Southeast
Sitka, AK 99835

Santa Rosa Junior College
Santa Rosa, CA 95409-6597

Colorado Northwest Community College
Rangeley, CO 81648

University of Massachusetts
Amherst, MA 01003

Vermilion Community College
Ely, MN 55731-1996

Southeastern Community College
Whiteville, NC 28472

Southwestern Community College
Franklin, NC 28734

APPENDIX 2

Cuyahoga Community College
Parma, OH 44130

Hocking College
Nelsonville, OH 45764-9508

Slippery Rock University
Slippery Rock, PA 16057-1326

Western Dakota VoTech Institute
Rapid City, SD 57701-4187

Memphis State University
Memphis, TN 38152

Walters State Community College
Morristown, TN 37813-6899

Skagit Valley College
Mount Vernon, WA 98273-5899

University of Maine-Presque Isle
Presque Isle, ME 04769-2888

Appendix 3
Pay Scales

In several chapters, we have talked about GS-7 and WG-3 and other grade levels. But what do these levels mean in terms of cash? GS stands for General Schedule and covers professional, administrative, clerical, and technical jobs. Other work such as firefighting and law enforcement are included in the GS series. WG stands for Wage Grade and covers trades, crafts, and manual labor.

Following are the federal GS pay scale and one example of a WG pay rate for 1995. The GS pay rates are fairly standard across the country, although federal employees in a few large cities and in Alaska receive a pay differential ranging from 8 to 25 percent to attract workers to these high-cost areas. Generally a GS-11 resource manager at Yosemite National Park earns the same salary as his or her counterpart at Cape Cod National Seashore.

The WG rates are tied to the pay scales of the local area. A carpenter in rural Shenandoah National Park could be expected to earn a wage comparable to that of a carpenter in the area but not as much as a carpenter at Golden Gate National Recreation Area in San Francisco. Approximately 150 areas have their own WG rates, including all the states and many large cities. Salary surveys are done each year for the WG pay rates. The WG rate given is for the Wichita Falls, Texas, area.

Appendix 3

Both the GS and WG rates can be expected to increase each year by a 2 to 4 percent cost-of-living raise established by the President and Congress.

There are ten in-grade steps in the GS series and five in the WG series. Your pay is determined first by your grade level and second by which step you have reached in that grade. On the General Schedule table, if you were hired as a GS-7, you would start at Step 1 making $24,038 per year. Based on good annual performance ratings, you would receive yearly step increases up to Step 4. From Step 4 to Step 7, the step increases would come every two years, and from Step 7 through Step 10, every three years.

In the Wage Grades, you can go from Step 1 to Step 2 in 26 weeks. Step 2 to Step 3 takes 78 weeks; Step 3 to Step 4 and Step 4 to Step 5 each takes 104 weeks.

Wage Grade Rates for Meridian, Mississippi for 1995

Grade	Steps 1	2	3	4	5
1	7.75	8.07	8.39	8.72	9.04
2	8.46	8.81	9.16	9.51	9.87
3	9.16	9.54	9.92	10.30	10.68
4	9.86	10.27	10.68	11.09	11.50
5	10.56	11.00	11.44	11.88	12.32
6	11.27	11.74	12.21	12.68	13.15
7	11.97	12.47	12.97	13.47	13.97
8	12.67	13.20	13.73	14.26	14.78
9	13.37	13.93	14.49	15.04	15.60
10	14.08	14.67	15.26	15.84	16.43
11	14.78	15.40	16.02	16.63	17.25
12	15.48	16.13	16.78	17.42	18.07
13	16.19	16.86	17.53	18.21	18.88
14	16.85	17.56	18.27	18.96	19.69
15	17.53	18.23	18.97	19.72	20.45

Appendix

General Schedule Pay Rates for 1995

Grade	Step 1	2	3	4	5	6	7	8	9	10
GS-1	$12,595	$13,015	$13,433	$13,851	$14,272	$14,517	$14,929	$15,346	$15,365	$15,751
2	14,161	14,498	14,968	15,365	15,534	15,990	16,447	16,903	17,360	17,816
3	15,452	15,968	16,483	16,999	17,514	18,030	18,546	19,061	19,577	20,092
4	17,346	17,924	18,502	19,080	19,658	20,236	20,813	21,391	21,969	22,547
5	19,407	20,054	20,701	21,349	21,996	22,643	23,291	23,938	24,585	25,233
6	21,632	22,353	23,074	23,795	24,516	25,237	25,958	26,679	27,400	28,121
7	24,038	24,838	25,639	26,440	27,241	28,042	28,843	29,644	30,445	31,245
8	26,622	27,509	28,396	29,283	30,170	31,057	31,944	32,831	33,718	34,605
9	29,405	30,385	31,366	32,346	33,326	34,307	35,287	36,268	37,248	38,228
10	32,382	33,462	34,542	35,622	36,702	37,782	38,862	39,942	41,022	42,102
11	35,578	36,763	37,949	39,135	40,321	41,506	42,692	43,878	45,064	46,249
12	42,641	44,063	45,484	46,905	48,326	49,747	51,169	52,590	54,011	55,432
13	50,706	52,396	54,086	55,776	57,466	59,156	60,846	62,536	64,225	65,915
14	59,920	61,917	63,914	65,911	67,908	69,905	71,902	73,899	75,896	77,893
15	70,482	72,832	75,181	77,531	79,881	82,231	84,580	86,930	89,280	91,629

Appendix 3

General Schedule Pay Rates for 1996

	Step-1	2	3	4	5	6	7	8	9	10
GS-1	$13,132	$13,570	$14,006	$14,442	$14,880	$15,136	$15,566	$16,000	$16,019	$16,425
2	14,764	15,116	15,606	16,019	16,197	16,673	17,149	17,625	18,101	18,577
3	16,111	16,647	17,184	17,720	18,257	18,793	19,330	19,867	20,403	20,940
4	18,085	18,688	19,292	19,895	20,499	21,102	21,705	22,309	22,912	23,515
5	20,233	20,908	21,582	22,257	22,931	23,606	24,280	24,954	25,629	26,303
6	22,554	23,305	24,057	24,809	25,561	26,313	27,065	27,816	28,568	29,320
7	25,061	25,897	26,733	27,568	28,404	29,239	30,075	30,911	31,746	32,582
8	27,756	28,682	29,607	30,533	31,459	32,385	33,310	34,236	35,162	36,088
9	30,658	31,681	32,703	33,725	34,747	35,769	36,792	37,814	38,836	39,858
10	33,762	34,887	36,012	37,137	38,262	39,387	40,513	41,638	42,763	43,888
11	37,094	38,330	39,567	40,803	42,040	43,276	44,512	45,749	46,985	48,222
12	44,458	45,941	47,423	48,906	50,388	51,871	53,353	54,835	56,318	57,800
13	52,867	54,630	56,392	58,154	59,917	61,679	63,442	65,204	66,966	68,729
14	62,473	64,556	66,639	68,721	70,804	72,887	74,969	77,052	79,134	81,217
15	73,486	75,935	78,385	80,834	83,284	85,733	88,183	90,632	93,082	95,531

THE WASHINGTON POST

For Further Reading

Albright, Horace M., and Cahn, Robert. *The Birth of the National Park Service: The Founding Years, 1913–33*. Salt Lake City and Chicago: Howe Brothers, 1985.

Butcher, Devereaux. *Exploring Our National Parks and Monuments*, 8th ed. Cambridge and Boston: Harvard Common Press, 1985.

Everhart, William C. *The National Park Service*. New York: Praeger Publishers, 1972.

Garrison, Lemuel A. *The Making of a Ranger: Forty Years with the National Parks*. Salt Lake City: Howe Brothers; Sun Valley, ID: Institute of the American West, 1983.

Hartzog, George B., Jr. *Battling for the National Parks*. Mt. Kisco, NY: Moyer Bell, 1988.

Muir, John. *Our National Parks*. Madison: University of Wisconsin Press, 1981.

National Park Service Careers. Washington, DC: U.S. Department of the Interior, National Park Service, 1989.

A Personal Training Program for Interpreters. Washington, DC: National Park Service, Division of Interpretation, 1976.

Pyne, Stephen J. *Fire in America: A Cultural History of Wildland and Rural Fire*. Princeton, NJ: Princeton University Press, 1982.

For Further Reading

———. *Fire on the Rim: A Firefighter's Season at the Grand Canyon.* New York: Weidenfeld & Nicolson, 1989.
Runte, Alfred. *National Parks: The American Experience,* 2d. rev. Lincoln: University of Nebraska Press, 1987.
Schullery, Paul. *Mountain Time.* New York: Schocken Books, 1984.
———. *The National Parks: The Classic Book on the National Parks, National Monuments and Historic Sites,* 3d rev. ed. New York: Knopf, 1986.
Sholly, Dan R. *Guardians of Yellowstone.* New York: Morrow, 1991.
Tilden, Freeman. *Interpreting Our Heritage,* 3d ed. Chapel Hill: University of North Carolina Press, 1977.
Wauer, Roland H. *The Role of the National Park Service Natural Resources Manager.* Seattle: National Park Service, Cooperative Park Studies Unit, College of Forest Resources, University of Washington, 1980.
Wirth, Conrad L. *Parks, Politics, and the People.* Norman: University of Oklahoma Press, 1980.

Index

A
Administrative Careers With America (ACWA), 170
Albright Training Center, 175
Amistad National Recreation Area, 102
Apostle Islands National Lakeshore, 120
archeologist, 117–122
architects, 81–85
Arlington National Cemetery, 9
assistant superintendent (AS), 28, 32–33
Association of National Park Rangers (ANPR), 4
Aviation Unit, Park Police, 45–46

B
backcountry rangers, 65–73
bears, 25–26, 68–69, 72
Big Bend National Park, 22
Big Cypress National Preserve, xvi
Blue Ridge Parkway, xvi, 19
Boise InterAgency Fire Center, xiii, 153
Border Patrol, 24
Bryce Canyon National Park, 61
budgeting, 32, 34, 56–57, 178, 179–180
Buildings and Utilities (B&U), 59
Bureau of Land Management, 163, 174

C
campsites/campgrounds, 25, 67–68, 81, 84, 124
Canine Unit, Park Police, 50
Canyonlands National Park, 106, 176
Cape Hatteras National Seashore, 8
Carlsbad Canyon National Park, 61
Chaco Culture National Historic Park, 8, 33
Chesapeake and Ohio Canal National Historic Park, xiv
clerk-typist, 37–40, 175
concessions, 145–149, 159, 174
  management specialists, 145–149
Conference of National Park Concessioners, 159, 174
Congress, 30, 75, 76, 78, 177
contracting officer representative (COR), 83, 85
Cooperative Park Studies Units (CPSU), 96
craftsmen, 59
Criminal Investigations Branch, 46–47
Cumberland Gap National Historical Park, 110
Cuyahoga Valley National Recreation Area, 37

D
Denver Service Center, 81–85
dispatchers, 123–127
Drug Recognition Expert program, 48

E
ecological issues, 2
emergency medical services (EMS), 72, 104
enabling legislation, 75
engineers, 59, 81–85

193

INDEX

environmental laws, 2
Environmental Protection Agency, 63
Everglades National Park, 27, 29, 95, 96, 106, 136–140, 158, 176

F
fatalities, in parks, 108
federal job, applying for, 167–171
Federal Job Information Centers (FJIC), 167, 170
Federal Law Enforcement Training Center (FLETC), 19, 21, 52, 153, 178
Field Training Officer Program, 52
Fire in America: A Cultural History of Wildland and Rural Fire, 134
fire management, 129–134
firefighting, 71, 129, 132–134
red card, 131
fishing, 29, 95
Florissant Fossil Beds, 153–154
Fort Jefferson, 114, 120
franchise fee, 146, 149
Fredericksburg and Spotsylvania County National Military Park, 24–25, 111
Freedom of Information Act (FOIA), 141
Freeman Tilden Award, 8
funding, park, 30, 97

G
Gateway National Recreation Area, 2, 42, 174
General Management Plan (GMP), 28, 76, 78, 83, 146
George Washington's Birthplace National Monument, 13, 88
Gettysburg National Military Park, 8, 87
Glacier National Park, 31, 65, 96
Glen Canyon National Recreation Area, 33, 102

Glen Echo Park, 9
Golden Gate National Recreation Area, xvi, 42, 174
Grand Canyon National Park, 16, 28, 31, 83, 102, 106, 122, 146
Grand Teton National Park, 102, 123, 127, 176
Grants Grade Evaluations (GGE), 98–99
Great Smoky Mountains National Park, 25, 27, 96, 110
"green bloods", xii

H
High School Volunteer Program, 163
historians, 109–115
Historic Structure Reports, 110
historic zone, 79
historical parks, 110
Horsemounted Unit, Park Police, 43–44, 45

I
Incident Command System (ICS), 102–103, 130, 138
Incident Commander, 126, 130
Independence National Historical Park, 174
Indiana Dunes National Lakeshore, 1, 19, 28, 84, 102, 178
Interpreting Our Heritage, 10
interpretive rangers, 7–17, 88, 108, 113, 151, 152
historians, 110, 114, 115
Investigators Annual Report, 99
Isle Royale National Park, 120

J
Joshua Tree National Monument, xii, 103, 158, 178

L
Lake Mead Amistad Recreation Area, 102, 104

INDEX

land ownership, 77
landscape architects, 59, 81–85
law enforcement rangers, 19–26, 151, 152, 153
commissions, 19–21, 70
living history program, 13–14, 110
Lyndon B. Johnson Natural Historic Site, xiv

M

Maintenance Management (MM) program, 56–57
maintenance workers, 55–64, 88, 113, 152
Mammoth Cave National Park, 89, 93
Mather Training Center, 91, 155, 175
media relations, 137, 139–140
Memorandums of Understanding (MOUS), 103
Midwest Archeological Center, 117
Motor Unit, Park Police, 50–51
Mount Rainier National Park, 84, 102, 106, 176

N

Narcotics/Vice Unit, Park Police, 46–47
Natchez Trace Parkway, 19
National Crime Information Center (NCIC), 125
National Historic Landmarks, 111
National Historic Preservation Act, 111
National Institutes of Health, 97
National Interagency Coordination Center (NICC), 131
national park, designating, 75–76
National Park Service (NPS), xi-xvi, 1–2, 27, 37
applying with, 167–171, 173–180
mission, 2, 9, 122, 145
National Parks Visitor Facilities and Services, 159

National Register of Historic Places, 111, 118
National Science Foundation, 97
National Trails Program, 76
natural zone, 79
New River Gorge National River, 104

O

Office of Personnel Management (OPM), 167, 169–170
Old Faithful, 29
Olympic National Park, 14

P

Padre Island National Seashore, 102
park development zone, 79
park management zones, 79–80
park planners, 75–80
Park Police, 41–53
Park Service Incident Commander, 104
Park Watchmen, 41
pay scales
clerk-typist, 39, 175
concession employees, 159
maintenance workers, 59–60
rangers, 2, 3, 5
research scientists, 98
seasonal employees, 158–159
permits,
backcountry, 67, 70
cave, 90
commercial film, 140–141
poaching, xi, 1, 24, 25, 69–70, 89
Point Reyes National Seashore, xiv
pollution, 29
prescribed fires, 131–132
Public Affairs (PA) Officer, 135–143

R

Ranger Rendezvous, 4
rangers, 1–5
backcountry, 65–73

195

INDEX

interpretive, 7–17, 88, 108, 113, 114, 115
law enforcement, 19–26, 70
rescue, 101–108
red card, 131
regulated monopoly, 147
rescue rangers, 101–108
research, 95, 96
  study standards, 97–98
  historians, 110, 112
Research Grade Evaluation (RGE), 98
Resource Assistant Program, 163–165
resource management, 71, 87–93, 130, 152, 176
  cultural, 62, 87, 114, 152
  natural, 62, 87, 152
Roads and Trails (R&T), 59
Rocky Mountain National Park, 8, 51, 158

S

St. Croix National Scenic Riverway, 96, 158
search-and-rescue (SAR), 102–108, 125–126, 130, 136
seasonal employees, 157–159, 173
secretary, 37–40
Sequoia National Park, 83
scenic parks, 110
scientists, 95–99
Shenandoah National Park, 25, 29, 63, 88, 95
Shiloh, 8
site survey, 118
Sleeping Bear Dunes National Lakeshore, xiv, 158
South Florida Research Center, 96
Southwest Cultural Resources Center, 118, 120
special use zones, 80
Special Weapons and Assault Team (SWAT), Park Police, 47, 48
Speed Enforcement Program, 48

Statement for Interpretation, 8
structural fires, 132–134
Student Conservation Association (SCA), 72, 73, 163, 165
superintendents, park, 27–35, 152
  assistant, 31
  functions, 33–34
survey, reconnaissance, 76–77

T

Tilden, Freeman, 7
Timpanogos Cave National Monument, 61
tourism, 141
traffic control, 22
Traffic Safety Unit, Park Police, 48
training, 151–155, 175
  dispatchers, 127
  firefighting, 129, 153, 175
  interpretive rangers, 14–15, 175
  law enforcement, 19–20, 153
  park police, 52
  public affairs officer, 142
  resource management, 154
  specialists, 154–155, 180
  volunteers, 162
"tree huggers", xii

U

Uplands Research Center, 96
U.S. Army, 1
U.S. Cavalry, xi, 1, 65
U.S. Department of the Interior, xii, 41, 113, 143
U.S. Fish and Wildlife Service (FWS), 25, 90, 163, 174
U.S. Forest Service, 163, 174

V

veteran preferences, 170
Vicksburg National Military park, 109
Virgin Islands, 158
visitors centers, 13, 79, 81, 124
Volunteers in Parks (VIPs), 14, 16,

196

INDEX

157, 161–165, 173
Voyageurs National Park, 119

W
Wild and Scenic Rivers Program, 76
wildland fires, 129–132
Williamsport Preservation Training Center (WPTC), 153

Y
Yellowstone National Park, xii, 25, 69, 87, 96, 102,
fire, 72, 129–130, 135–136
managing, 28, 29, 34, 136, 138–140, 176
wolves in, 30–31, 95
Yosemite National Park, 3, 8, 22, 68, 101, 102, 104
managing, 28, 66, 146, 176
Youth Conservation Corps (YCC), 63, 72, 73

Z
Zion National Park, 51